APT Initiatives

ESSENTIAL REVISION POCKETBOOK

for AQA AS Business Studies Students

Unit 2 (BUSS2): MANAGING A BUSINESS

by **Claire Baker**

Consolidating Learning and Simplifying Revision

© **APT Initiatives Limited**, 2011

Author: **Claire Baker**

All rights reserved. No part of this publication may be reproduced, stored in or introduced into a retrieval system, or transmitted, in any form, or by any means (electronic, mechanical, photocopying, recording or otherwise) without the written permission of APT Initiatives Ltd, or under licence from the Copyright Licensing Agency Limited, of 90 Tottenham Court Road, London W1P 9HE. Any person who does any unauthorised act in relation to this publication may be liable to criminal prosecution and civil claims for damages.

A CIP catalogue record for this book is available from the British Library.

ISBN: 978-0-9556408-7-2

Published by

APT Initiatives Limited
Millstone Lodge
Eaton Upon Tern
Market Drayton
Shropshire
TF9 2BX

Tel: 01952 540877
Fax: 01952 541230
email:sales@apt-initiatives.com
www.apt-initiatives.com

Cover illustration ©iStockphoto.com

Printed and bound by Think Ink, Ipswich, Suffolk, UK

FOREWORD

This Essential Revision Pocketbook has been produced for students of AQA GCE AS / A Level Business Studies. It covers the essential theory required for the GCE Business Studies specification for AQA AS Unit 2 (BUSS2): Managing a Business. It contains all the information students need to consolidate their learning and simplify revision.

For each of the core topic areas and individual sub-topic areas listed in the unit specification there are definitions of key terms and concise coverage of the relevant Business Studies theory and concepts. Care has been taken to ensure the information provided is accurate, up-to-date and precise, and directly matches the requirements of the unit specification. The pocketbook also provides a highly comprehensive explanation of the skills examiners look for when marking students' answers and how to demonstrate these skills, as well as other essential advice on how to maximise performance in the examination.

The author, Claire Baker, is an experienced teacher, examiner, author and the owner and Managing Director of APT Initiatives Limited. She has taught Business Studies from ages 11 to 19 and has been an examiner, Principal Examiner and Reviser for Business Studies and Business related courses for a leading awarding body.

This Revision Pocketbook is a condensed version of APT Initiatives Ltd's 'Elementary Explanations' written by Claire Baker, which provides in-depth coverage of the essential theory required by the Unit 2 (BUSS2) specification.

A range of activities to test and develop students' knowledge and understanding of the Business Studies theory and concepts covered in both these textbooks is provided in other resources available from APT Initiatives Ltd.

APT Initiatives Ltd can be contacted directly with any orders, queries or feedback via the website: www.apt-initiatives.com, via email: support@apt-initiatives.com or by phone: 01952 540877.

CONTENTS

FINANCE

USING BUDGETS — 2

The Benefits and Drawbacks of Using Budgets
The Calculation and Interpretation of Variances
Using Variance Analysis to Inform Decision-making

IMPROVING CASH FLOW — 6

Causes of Cash Flow Problems
Methods of Improving Cash Flow

MEASURING AND INCREASING PROFIT — 10

The Calculation and Understanding of Net Profit Margins
The Calculation and Understanding of Return on Capital
Methods of Improving Profits / Profitability
The Distinction between Cash and Profit

PEOPLE IN BUSINESS

IMPROVING ORGANISATIONAL STRUCTURES — 14

Key Elements of Organisational Structure
Workforce Roles
How Organisational Structure Affects Business Performance

MEASURING THE EFFECTIVENESS OF THE WORKFORCE — 19

Methods of Measuring Workforce Performance

DEVELOPING AN EFFECTIVE WORKFORCE: RECRUITMENT, SELECTION, TRAINING — 22

The Recruitment Process
Internal and External Recruitment
Selecting the Best Employees
How Recruitment & Selection can Improve a Workforce
Methods of Training

DEVELOPING AN EFFECTIVE WORKFORCE: MOTIVATING EMPLOYEES — 28

Motivation – An Introduction
Theories of Motivation
Using Financial Methods to Motivate Employees
Improving Job Design
Empowering Employees
Working in Teams

OPERATIONS MANAGEMENT

MAKING OPERATIONAL DECISIONS — 36

Operational Targets
Calculating and Managing Capacity Utilisation
Operational Issues Dealing with Non-standard Orders and Matching Production and Demand

© APT Initiatives Ltd, 2011

DEVELOPING EFFECTIVE OPERATIONS: QUALITY — 41	**DESIGNING AN EFFECTIVE MARKETING MIX** — 53

DEVELOPING EFFECTIVE OPERATIONS: QUALITY — 41

The Meaning and Importance of Quality
The Distinction between Quality Control and Quality Assurance
Systems of Quality Assurance
Quality Standards

DEVELOPING EFFECTIVE OPERATIONS: CUSTOMER SERVICE — 44

Methods of Meeting Customer Expectations
Monitoring and Improving Customer Service
The Benefits of High Levels of Customer Service

WORKING WITH SUPPLIERS — 46

Choosing Effective Suppliers
The Role in Improving Operational Performance

USING TECHNOLOGY IN OPERATIONS — 47

Types & Benefits of Technology in Operations Management
Issues in Introducing and Updating Technology

MARKETING AND THE COMPETITIVE ENVIRONMENT

EFFECTIVE MARKETING — 51

The Purpose of Marketing
Niche and Mass Marketing
Consumer Marketing & Business to Business Marketing

DESIGNING AN EFFECTIVE MARKETING MIX — 53

Influences on the Marketing Mix
The Importance of an Integrated Mix

USING THE MARKETING MIX: PRODUCT — 55

Influences on the Development of New Goods & Services
Unique Selling Points (or Propositions)
Product Portfolio Analysis
Product Life Cycles

USING THE MARKETING MIX: PROMOTION — 59

Elements of the Promotional Mix
Influences on the Choice of Promotional Mix

USING THE MARKETING MIX: PRICING — 66

Price and Influences on Pricing Decisions
Pricing Strategies
Pricing Tactics

USING THE MARKETING MIX: PLACE — 70

Types of Distribution Channel, Outlets / Distributors
Factors Influencing Choice of Distribution Channel, Outlet / Distributor

MARKETING AND COMPETITIVENESS — 74

The Possible Impacts of Market Conditions and Degree of Competition
Determinants of Competitiveness
Methods of Improving Competitiveness

© APT Initiatives Ltd, 2011

MAXIMISING YOUR PERFORMANCE IN THE EXAMINATION

Summary of AQA GCE (AS/A) Level Mark Schemes	80
Individual Assessment Objectives Explained	81
Key Words & Phrases to Build 'Higher Level' Answers	84
Command Words and Appropriate Responses	85
The Structure of the Examination Paper	85
Top Tips to Maximise Your Performance	86

© **APT Initiatives Ltd**, 2011

FINANCE

USING BUDGETS

The Benefits and Drawbacks of Using Budgets

Budgets: agreed plans of action over a given period of time, eg 12 months, expressed in numerical terms. They concern targets relating to income, expenditure and profit, but may also concern planned activity levels, eg hours to be worked, units to be produced.

Income budgets: planned targets for revenue or other income streams (eg interest on investments) for a business, division or department in a given period of time.

Expenditure budgets: planned targets for spending or costs for a business, division or department in a given period of time.

Profit budgets: targets for profit ie income less expenditure for a business, division or department in a given period of time.

Example: Planned Income, Expenditure and Profit Budget for a Business over a 6 Month Period

Income Budget	Sept	Oct	Nov	Dec	Jan	Feb	Total
Sales	£48,000	£40,000	£32,000	£28,000	£28,000	£24,000	£200,000

Expenditure Budget	Sept	Oct	Nov	Dec	Jan	Feb	Total
Salaries	£6,000	£6,000	£6,000	£6,000	£6,000	£6,000	£36,000
Rent	£2,000	£2,000	£2,000	£2,000	£2,000	£2,000	£12,000
Advertising	£1,500	£1,500	£1,500	£500	£500	£500	£6,000
Fees/Subscriptions	£768	£640	£512	£448	£448	£384	£3,200
Utilities			£1,375			£1,375	£2,750
Insurance	£300	£300	£300	£300	£300	£300	£1,800
Telephone/Broadband			£810			£540	£1,350
Office Supplies	£300	£250	£200	£175	£175	£150	£1,250
Travel	£276	£230	£184	£161	£161	£138	£1,150
Total Expenses	**£11,144**	**£10,920**	**£12,811**	**£9,584**	**£9,584**	**£11,387**	**£65,500**

Profit Budget	Sept	Oct	Nov	Dec	Jan	Feb	Total
Income	£48,000	£40,000	£32,000	£28,000	£28,000	£24,000	£200,000
Expenses	£11,144	£10,920	£12,811	£9,584	£9,584	£11,387	£65,500
Profit	**£36,856**	**£29,080**	**£19,189**	**£18,416**	**£18,416**	**£12,613**	**£134,500**

© APT Initiatives Ltd, 2011

Benefits of Using Budgets:

Budgets provide clear targets for staff to achieve. This can help a business to:

- **maximise revenues** (income budgets).
- **control spending** and **minimise / reduce costs** (expenditure budgets).
- ensure **resources are used in the most efficient way**.
- ensure appropriate resources are allocated to projects to **meet the set targets.**
- maximise **profit and return on investment** and **meet objectives** relating to these (profit budgets).
- effectively **manage cash flow** (cash budgets).
- minimise **potential conflict** and **enhance teamwork**.
- allow **delegation without loss of control**.
- **identify and correct problems** at an early stage by providing a yardstick against which to measure actual performance.
- **motivate staff** – providing a sense of achievement if the target figures are met.

Overall, budgets **provide direction** and **aid motivation, co-ordination and control.**

They are particularly beneficial when a business **increases in size and complexity**, as control and co-ordination become more difficult.

Drawbacks of Using Budgets & Pitfalls to Avoid:

Failure to consult the key people involved in the achievement of budgeted figures can lead to **unrealistic targets** and **resentment and conflict with management**.

External, uncontrollable, often unforeseeable factors can affect the accuracy of the budgeted figures.

Used too rigidly budgets can **work against the achievement of business objectives** – for example by:

- restricting finance available to meet changing customer / business needs.
- stifling initiative resulting in slow reaction to change and missed business opportunities.
- containing unrealistic targets, leading to staff resentment.

In any of the scenarios, the use of budgets might **de-motivate rather than motivate staff**.

Avoiding the Pitfalls / Drawbacks:

To ensure appropriate, realistic targets are set (ie relevant and challenging yet achievable) and to minimise potential conflict:

- budgets should be based on accurate forecasts of demand.
- qualified, experienced individuals, who have responsibility for managing the budget and ensuring targets are achieved, should be consulted on what the figures should be.
- changes in the business environment that affect items listed in the budget should be regularly monitored, and figures adjusted accordingly to ensure they remain challenging yet achievable.

The Calculation and Interpretation of Favourable and Adverse Variances

Variance: the difference between the budgeted and actual figures.

Favourable variances: when actual figures are better than budgeted, eg when actual costs are less than budgeted costs, actual sales are more than budgeted sales, actual profit is more than budgeted profit.

Adverse variances: when actual figures are worse than budgeted, eg when actual costs are more than budgeted costs, actual sales are less than budgeted sales, actual profit is lower than budgeted profit.

Calculation: Subtract the budgeted figure from the actual figure, eg:

- Budgeted sales £290. Actual sales £360. Variance = £360 - £290 = + £70.
- Budgeted material cost £105. Actual cost £126. Variance = £126 - £105 = + £21.
- Budgeted profit £47. Actual profit £90. Variance = £90 - £47 = + £43.

To express the variance as a percentage: Divide the difference between the actual and budgeted figure into the budgeted figure, and multiply by 100, eg:

- Sales percentage variance = + £70 / £290 x 100 = + 24%
- Material cost percentage variance = + £21 / £105 x 100 = + 20%
- Profit percentage variance = + £43 / £47 x 100 = + 91%.

Interpretation:

- Sales variance (+ £70, 24%): **Favourable** – actual sales more than budgeted.

- Material cost variance (+ £21, 20%): **Adverse** – actual costs more than budgeted.

- Profit variance (+£43, 91%): **Favourable** – actual profit more than budgeted.

Possible Reasons for Favourable Variances in General:

Why Sales Might be Higher than Planned	Why Costs Might be Lower then Planned
Inaccurate budgeted figures eg due to: poor / inadequate research; calculation errors.	**Inaccurate budgeted figures** eg due to: poor / inadequate research; calculation errors.
Higher demand than expected (despite adequate research) eg due to: closure of competitor; more effective promotion.	**Reduced cost of materials / supplies** eg due to: supplier discounts on larger orders; fewer staff errors arising from improvements in training, motivation, or new machinery.
Fewer machine / equipment breakdowns - enabling greater output than planned eg due to new machinery.	**Less overtime or fewer staff employed** eg due to: reduced absence, labour turnover, improved motivation arising from improvements in training, pay or other benefits; automation.
Improvements in the motivation and ability of staff eg due to improvements in training, pay or other rewards.	

Possible Reasons for Adverse Variances in General:

Why Sales Might be Lower than Planned	Why Costs Might be Higher then Planned
• **Inaccurate budgeted figures** eg due to: poor / inadequate research; calculation errors. • **Lower demand than expected** (despite adequate research) eg due to: a new competitor; an increase in interest or income tax rates reducing the disposable income customers have to spend on the business's products / services; inadequate / ineffective promotional activities. • **Machine / equipment breakdowns** – less output than planned can be achieved, eg due to: failure to invest in new machinery; lack of planned, preventative maintenance; power cuts. • **Problems in securing labour** (with the right motivation and ability) **required** to produce the planned output, eg due to: poor recruitment, selection, induction, training, supervision, pay and / or other rewards and working conditions.	• **Inaccurate budgeted figures** eg due to: poor / inadequate research; calculation errors. • **Increased cost of materials / supplies** eg due to: suppliers putting up prices; increased errors / mistakes as new staff take time to become efficient and / or inadequate supervision, training and / or motivation of new and / or existing staff; theft / pilferage - inadequate security; errors in stock calculations / valuations. • **More overtime used or staff employed** because of unexpected staff absence, falling motivation and productivity as a result of weaknesses in human resource policy, procedures and practices. • **Unforeseen expenditure** eg machinery / equipment failure / breakage resulting in increased maintenance / equipment costs.

Using Variance Analysis to Inform Decision-making

Variance analysis: involves comparing and calculating differences between budgeted and actual figures and investigating possible reasons for any differences.

Decision-making: involves making a choice between alternative courses of action.

Variance Analysis: finds answers to the following...
1. Is the variance favourable or adverse?
2. What is the size of the variance?
3. Is the variance significant (particularly in % terms)? *If so, undertake an investigation to determine...*
4. To what extent was the variance predictable?
5. To what extent is it the result of factors beyond the company's control, and to what extent is it the result of failings within the organisation? *If the latter...*
6. Where do responsibilities lie?

Once this investigation and analysis has been undertaken **informed decisions** can then be made over what action should be taken, eg for a significant adverse cost variance due to an increase in the cost of raw materials, the firm can investigate and make decisions about alternatives, eg alternative suppliers.

IMPROVING CASH FLOW

Causes of Cash Flow Problems

Cash-flow: movement of money into and out of a business, including receipts and payments made by cash, cheques, debit cards, credit cards, direct debit or other credit transfer.

Cash inflows: cash coming into the business (receipts), including sales made in cash during the period, cash paid on previous credit sales, loans from the bank, grants from the government, interest on any investments.

Cash outflows: cash going out of the business (payments) including purchases of raw materials paid for in cash or cash paid for previous purchases made on credit, purchase of new machinery or equipment, expenses payable during the period eg on wages, rent, interest on loans, as well as any taxes.

Negative cash flow: where cash outflows exceed cash inflows.

Debtors: individuals or other businesses who owe the business money for goods or services received.

Creditors: individuals or other businesses to whom the business owes money (mostly suppliers of goods and / or services received but not yet paid for).

Stock (inventory): raw materials and components, work in progress or finished goods a business holds at any one time.

Overtrading: occurs when a firm expands its order book without generating sufficient cash in time to meet debts as they fall due.

- **Allowing too much credit**.
- **Negotiating too little credit** (in relation to credit granted to customers).
- **Poor credit control** eg failure to undertake credit checks, late invoicing / statementing, being slow to chase late payments.
- **Over-reliance on one or two customers** – can be a major problem if a significant amount is owed.
- **Holding excessive stock** – ties up cash <u>and</u> incurs costs.
- **Lack of budgeting and forecasting / poor financial planning** eg failure to plan VAT, PAYE and / or corporation tax payments.
- **Pre-occupation with growth and expansion** resulting in…
- …**over-trading** – securing new custom but neglecting cash.
- …**over-investment in fixed assets** eg investing in more buildings / vehicles / equipment and leaving the business short of cash.
- …**over-financing / borrowing** eg taking out a loan but failing to generate the sales and cash required to meet loan payments.
- **Ineffective marketing** – resulting in failure to generate the sales and cash required to cover expenses as they fall due.
- **Poor control of costs** – resulting in higher expenditure, lower profit and, thus, less cash.
- **Failure to make a profit** – thus failure, in the long-term, to generate sufficient cash to meet debts as they fall due.
- **Seasonal demand** – resulting in cash shortage at certain times the year.
- **Negative changes in the external business environment** eg recession negatively affecting demand for a business's product / service and, thus, sales and cash received.

Methods of Improving Cash Flow

Overdraft: an arrangement between a business or individual and their bank or building society to withdraw more money from their account than is deposited in it, up to an agreed limit. Interest is charged on any amounts overdrawn.

Short term loan: a business is advanced a set figure and repays the amount over an agreed period of time ie usually within a year, at an agreed rate of interest.

Factoring: a business sells its debts to a third party (factoring company) who usually provide around 80% to 85% of the value of payments due by customers instantly, and deduct a fee (of, say, 5%) when the total debt is recovered.

Leasing: a business rents a fixed asset rather than purchasing it outright and ownership of the asset remains with the finance company.

Sale of assets: a business sells fixed assets (eg land, buildings, vehicles, machinery) that they own and no longer use, or that are not making enough contribution to the firm's profits, in order to provide an injection of cash into the business.

Sale and lease back: a business sells fixed assets (eg land, buildings, vehicles, machinery) that they own and then leases them back, ie by paying a monthly sum to the leasing company (often banks), in order to free up cash whilst retaining use of the asset.

Monitor & Control Cash through Budgets, Cash Flow Forecasts:

Budgets help to avoid overspending; forecasts identify cash shortages and enable timely decisions to be made and implemented to cope with the forecast shortages.

Secure an Overdraft / Increase Existing Overdraft:

Advantages	Disadvantages
• Generally simple and quick to arrange. • Flexible and convenient – can draw / repay within agreed limit without notice. • Relatively cheap in short-term – interest only charged on balance at end of day. • No security required (unlike loans).	• Expensive if used regularly for large amounts – interest usually charged between 2% & 4% over bank's base rate. • Repayable on demand ie can be recalled without notice.

Take Out Short Term Loan:

Advantages
• Relatively simple and quick to arrange – depending on financial history and collateral (if required), plus sound plans.   • Lower rate of interest than overdrafts.   • Not repayable on demand – thus less risky than overdrafts.   • Payments can be offset against tax.

Disadvantages
• Regular interest payments – increases costs, reduces profit.   • Less flexible and more expensive than overdrafts – repayments are fixed and on agreed dates, interest on whole sum, may also be early repayment charge.   • Security ie collateral may be required.

© **APT Initiatives Ltd**, 2011

Reduce the Figure for Debtors eg through:

Debt Factoring ie sell debts to a business (factor) that specialises in collecting debts in return for a fee (% of the value of debts).

Advantages	Disadvantages
• Immediate cash benefit, reducing overdraft / interest payments. • May enable discounts as a result of prompt payment to suppliers. • Less administration costs in chasing late payment. • Time freed up to spend on other activities. • Reduced uncertainty - as factor takes on risk of bad debts.	• Reduced revenue and profit margins. • Negative customer perception / reaction – customer may prefer to deal directly with the firm; may interpret use of debt factoring as an indication the firm is suffering cash flow problems, which could have a negative effect on sales.

Other Methods	Advantage(s)	Disadvantage(s)
Tighter credit control eg credit checks, more timely invoicing / statementing, tracking of debtors, faster chasing of late payments.	Less need for overdraft / interest payments.	Additional administration.
Shorter and / or stricter payment terms eg shorter credit periods, cash in advance / deposits, charging interest on late payments.	As above.	Risk losing customers to suppliers who offer better / less stringent credit terms.
Discounts for prompt payment eg 2-5% discount if pay in advance, on delivery, or within 7-14 days.	As above.	Reduces gross margins.

Extend Credit with Suppliers:

Advantage(s)
- Allows time to receive money from customers.

Disadvantage(s)
- Interest may be charged on overdue accounts.
- Potential loss of discounts for prompt payment.
- May jeopardise future access to credit.

Sale of Assets:

Advantages
- No interest charges as with overdrafts, short term loans.
- Greater capacity utilisation and profitability – if asset is under-utilised.

Disadvantages
- Loss of use of asset – ensure no longer required / sale will not restrict future flexibility and profitability.
- Can be difficult to sell fixed assets quickly – thus lower price than could be realised may be achieved.
- Reduces collateral available to offer as security for a loan – may be harder to raise finance through borrowing.

Sale and Lease Back:

Advantages
- Cash generated while use of asset maintained.
- Leasing provides flexibility as business needs change.
- Leasing provides scope to update to latest technology often with little extra cost.
- Some (leasing) agreements also include a service and maintenance package – reducing these costs.
- Leasing payments can also be offset against tax.

Disadvantages
- Committed to meeting regular loan payments.
- In the long-run will have effectively paid for the asset, yet will not own it.
- Reduces collateral available to offer as security for a loan – harder to raise finance through borrowing.

© **APT Initiatives Ltd**, 2011

Other Methods to Improve Cash Flow:

Delay or Cut Planned Expenditure:

Eg rent or lease rather than buy premises, vehicles, machinery outright.

Cut or Postpone Drawings or Dividends to Shareholders:

Depends on personal circumstances of business owner and attitude / likely reaction of shareholders (in ltd company).

Reduce Stock Levels:

Eg through advertising, price discounts, tighter stock control.

Frees up cash and reduces stock holding costs. *However…*

- Risk of stockout - depends on good working relationships with suppliers.
- May lose discounts on bulk purchases.

Reduce Time Taken to Get Goods to Market:

Minimises the cost of holding stocks and speeds up payment. *However…*

- Improving efficiency of production and distribution could be complex and costly in the short-run eg requiring investment in new machinery / replacing labour with machines – cost of new machinery, training and installation costs, plus redundancy payments.

Increase Profits:

Eg by increasing revenues without a proportionate increase in costs, or cutting costs without a proportionate fall in revenues.

Slower Growth:

If rapid growth is the cause, then reduce rate of growth to allow systems to develop to maintain effective control.

Diversify into Products / Services that Sell Throughout the Year:

Seasonal businesses may overcome cash shortages by building up a surplus of funds in the peak season and / or developing products and markets which ensure a more even inflow of cash throughout the year.

The most appropriate method for improving cash flow in a given situation will depend upon:

- **cause** of cash flow problem facing the business in question.

There are many factors outside a business's control that affect cash flows that are hard to predict. *Thus, it is a good idea to:*

- **keep some cash in reserve** just in case of late payments.
- **take out credit insurance** for any unexpected non-payment of debt.

MEASURING AND INCREASING PROFIT

The Calculation and Understanding of Net Profit Margins

> **Profit:** what is left from revenue after costs have been deducted.
>
> **Gross profit:** profit made before overheads (other running costs) are deducted from revenue - calculated by deducting the cost of sales (direct costs) from revenue (turnover).
>
> **Net profit** (profit before tax): profit made after cost of sales, other expenses and interest have been deducted from revenue, but before tax.
>
> **Profit margins:** look at the relationship between profit and revenue. They provide an indication of how effectively costs are being managed within a business.
>
> **Net profit margin:** measures what percentage of a business's revenue is net profit - calculated by dividing the net profit figure into revenue and multiplying by 100.

Calculation:

Net Profit / Revenue x 100 = X%

Example: A chair manufacturing business's revenue for the year is £320,000. Total costs (direct and overhead) for the year are £192,000. Net profit is:

- £128,000 (320,000 – 192,000).

The net profit margin is:

- 40% (128,000 / 320,000 x 100).

NB Net profit can be:

- Net profit before interest and tax (ie operating profit).
- Net profit after interest but before tax (ie profit before tax).
- Net profit after tax (profit for the year).

Understanding / Interpretation:

The margin should be compared to previous margins achieved by the business. The higher the percentage, the better the business is performing.

A fall in the net profit margin could be due to:

- a fall in revenues.
- a rise in cost of sales (direct costs).
- an increase in indirect costs (overheads).

An increase could be due to the reverse of any of the above.

NB It is difficult to make fair comparisons between businesses as operating and financial arrangements can differ considerably, resulting in different levels of expenditure. It is particularly unfair to make comparisons between industries, eg for supermarkets 4-7% is acceptable, for building a house 20-22% may be acceptable.

The Calculation and Understanding of Return on Capital

Capital: money invested in a business or specific business project - from owners and shareholders (equity or share capital) or from banks and building societies, or other financial institutions (loan capital).

Return on capital: a ratio expressing the amount of money made on an investment (the return) as a percentage of money invested (the capital). Sometimes referred to as the **'primary efficiency'** ratio - provides a direct measure of the main task of management, ie maximise return on capital invested in a business or a specific business project.

Calculation:

Return / Capital invested x 100 = X%

Example: a business invests £60,000 in a new machine which generates a return of £6,000. Return on capital will be:

10% (£6,000 / £60,000 x 100).

Understanding / Interpretation:

The ratio should be compared with previous years or similar entities / industry norms.
The higher the percentage, the better the business performance. A fall could be due to:

- fall in profit (arising from fall in revenues and / or rise in costs).
- increase in capital invested (without a proportionate rise in profit).

NB If a large proportion of capital invested is via loans the ROC should be sufficient to cover interest payable on loan(s) plus inflation. Otherwise, the business may as well close, sell off its assets and put the money in a bank.

Methods of Improving Profits / Profitability

Profit: what is left from revenue after costs have been deducted.

Profitability: relationship between profit and something else eg revenue (net margin) or capital invested (return on capital).

General Ways to Improve Profits / Profitability:

Improving Profits & Profitability in terms of Net Margins	Improving Profitability in terms of Return on Capital
• Increase revenue without increasing costs, or at a greater rate (percentage increase) than any increase in costs.	• Increase profit without increasing capital invested, or at a greater rate (percentage increase) than any increase in capital.
• Reduce costs without reducing revenues, or without a proportionate fall in revenue.	• Reduce capital invested without reducing profit, or without a proportionate fall in profit.
• Elements of both ie increase revenue <u>and</u> reduce costs.	• Elements of both ie increase profit <u>and</u> reduce capital.

© **APT Initiatives Ltd**, 2011

Increasing Revenues

Raising Prices

- Increases unit margin (unit selling price – unit costs).
- Simple, requires no change to operations. *However:*
- Could put off some customers - where close substitutes exist.

Increasing Sales Volumes

- Demand, thus, sales volume, might be increased by: favourable changes in environment eg closure of competitor; improving product, promotion, access (incur costs); **reducing prices** (reduces unit margin).

- Selling more will increase: *profit* - if extra costs do not exceed increase in revenue; *profitability* - if revenue increases at greater rate than costs.

- Profit/profitability may increase as: fixed costs spread over more units; if variable cost per unit falls from supplier discounts on larger orders.

- **Price reductions**: If fall in unit costs from higher volumes exceeds fall in unit selling price, then unit profit margin will be higher.

Cost Reduction

Shopping Around / Negotiating to Secure Best Prices

- Eg for materials, energy, telephone, advertising, bank, legal.
- Minor cost involved - time researching / negotiating.
- Ensure alternatives aren't secured at expense of quality.

Adopting Flexible Working Practices & Outsourcing

- Reduce wage bill through use of temporary, part-time staff.
- Reduce floor space, thus rent & rates through homeworking.
- Reduce wage bill through outsourcing non-core / critical activities. *But*…less control redundancies, effect on morale?

Investing in New Machinery / Equipment / Technology

- Automation, more efficient machinery, ICT may cut wages, water, energy, telephone, marketing and / or travel costs.

- May incur capital, installation & training costs. **But,** should be outweighed in longer-term through reduction in running costs.

The Distinction between Cash and Profit

> **Cash:** the amount of money held within a business's bank account and in hand at a particular moment in time.
> **Profit:** what is left from revenue after costs have been deducted.

- Sales £120,000, costs £85,000, profit = £35,000. But this may not all be held as cash. Some revenue may be owed by customers to whom firm allows credit. Firm may also have received goods for which it has not yet paid. Thus, may hold less/more cash than that equal to profit.

- A business might be fundamentally profitable but if cash does not flow in quickly enough to pay bills, unless additional cash funds can be raised, the business might be declared bankrupt and forced into liquidation by creditors.

- In the **short term cash is more essential than profit** - can survive without profit. *But* cannot borrow money forever. Owners / shareholders require some return on their investment and lenders need the debt to be eventually settled. Thus, **profit is essential for long term survival**.

PEOPLE IN BUSINESS

IMPROVING ORGANISATIONAL STRUCTURES

Key Elements of Organisational Structure

Organisational structure: the way in which an organisation's activities are grouped together and coordinated to ensure members work together to achieve organisational goals.

Hierarchy: the order of levels of management or supervision within a business, from lowest to highest.

Spans of control: the number of people reporting directly to a particular manager or supervisor (or the number of people for whom a manager or supervisor is directly responsible).

Job allocation: involves assigning specific tasks to specific individuals (or groups) within the organisation (or other businesses.

Work loads: tasks and duties that individuals (or groups) are expected to carry out in a given time period eg day, week, month.

Delegation: passing responsibility for undertaking a task or making a decision to subordinates ie employees at lower levels in the hierarchy.

Communication flows: directions in which information flows in relation to the organisational hierarchy ie vertical, lateral and diagonal.

Levels of Hierarchy:

In general, the more people, the more hierarchical. *Eg…*

- Local fruit / veg store may consist of 2 levels: owner-manager + sales staff.
- Large national company may have many levels →

Up to 3 = flat structure.

4 or more = tall, hierarchical, or pyramid structure.

MD
Directors
Senior Managers
Middle Managers
Junior Managers
Supervisors
Team leaders
Operatives

Spans of Control:

Manager
Employees

Span of control = **7**

In hierarchical structures span is usually narrow.

In flat structures span is generally wide.

The ideal span depends upon…

- **nature of the work carried out by workers.**
- **geographical spread of workers.**
- **variability of the work.**
- **amount of planning / organising** in allocating tasks.
- **tasks a supervisor performs as an individual.**
- **quality and competence of supervisor.**

Eg: If, work is simple and repetitive, workers are in the same location, work is not varied, the task of allocating work is reasonably straightforward, a span of control of 16 staff would probably not be too wide.

Job Allocation / Work Loads:

Job allocation requires careful analysis to ensure work loads are appropriate.

Involves **work measurement** to determine how much can be undertaken by an individual (or group) in a period of time.

Wide spans of control and a **lack of delegation** can increase workloads.

Delegation: To be effective…

- **Nature of the task should be clear.**
- **Delegate should be capable.**
- **Results expected and timing should be clear.**
- **Delegate must have sufficient authority.**
- **Those who need to know should be informed.**
- **Limitations should be made clear.**
- **Manager's ultimate responsibility should be made clear.**

Also requires: **trust** and **willingness** of **managers** to delegate.

Communication Flows:

Vertical communication:

Information flows from **upper** hierarchical levels **to lower** hierarchical levels (ie downwards), and **vice versa** (upwards).

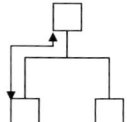

Downwards: used by management to give instructions, assign duties, provide general information to employees.

Upwards: used by employees to feedback, make suggestions, seek clarification, air grievances.

Lateral (horizontal) communication:

Communication **across** the organisation, ie between people at the same hierarchical level.

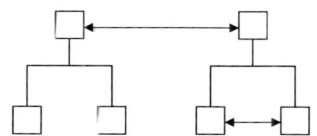

Eg: Research & Development informing Finance department of the costs of producing a new product.

Usually used to share information and ideas, solve problems, resolve conflict.

Diagonal communication:

Communication between people at **different** hierarchical **levels** within **different sections** of the business.

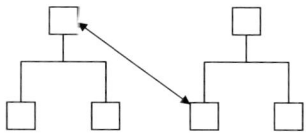

Eg: Marketing Manager giving instructions to a Production operative; Marketing assistant giving cost information to a Finance Director.

Often takes place on projects which involve several departments and there are no clear lines of authority, or employees are required to report to several managers in different departments.

Workforce Roles

Supervisor: a member of staff who has authority over one or several individuals or group of individuals within an organisation and is responsible for their performance on a day to day basis. It is the most junior managerial position within an organisation.

Team leader: a member of staff who has authority over a group of individuals within an organisation, who are required to work together cohesively in order to achieve a common (often) short term goal.

Manager: a member of staff who has authority over a number of other individuals or groups within an organisation and responsibility for planning, organising, monitoring and controlling the achievement of short to medium term goals.

Director: one of the most senior members of staff in an organisation who is elected by shareholders each year to represent their decisions and run the business on their behalf.

Supervisor:

- Ensure staff carry out tasks according to standards required on a daily basis.
- Should have the knowledge / experience required to advise / instruct staff, and resolve task related problems.
- Generally has power to decide how tasks should be divided and to change roles of group members.
- Does not generally have the power to hire, fire or promote. Recommends such action to the next level of management.

Team Leader:

- Ensures team goals are met, encourages and maintains group cohesion.
- May allocate tasks - taking into account individual strengths of team members.
- May select and appoint members to ensure the right blend of skills and personal qualities.
- May assign targets for individuals to achieve and evaluate performance against these.

Should...

- be capable of setting aims, targets, goals.
- use skills / qualities of individuals effectively.
- set an example through personal performance
- mediate, talk through problems, resolve them.
- initiate discussions and exchange of ideas.
- be supportive not dictatorial - allow members to lead discussions, try to ensure all make a contribution so decisions made are team ones.

Manager:

- In limited companies - appointed by directors to assist in day to day running.
- In small businesses owner may assume all managerial tasks. As business grows may appoint and delegate responsibility to managers, as control becomes more difficult for one person to maintain.
- Rely on owners / directors to support decisions and is held accountable if workers are inefficient.

Director:

- Concerned with strategic direction – responsible for setting / overseeing medium to long-term goals.
- May appoint managers to assist them and to make operational and tactical decisions on their behalf.
- Often hold shares in the companies they run.
- **Executive directors:** employees of the business, usually responsible for running a large division.
- **Non-executive directors:** not employees, usually experienced senior managers from other firms, appointed to give independent advice.

How Organisational Structure Affects Performance

Business performance: concerns a business's ability to:
- fulfil its function / achieve its overall purpose, mission, aims & objectives.
- control costs, maximise sales and profits and meet short, medium and long-term targets relating to these.
- meet needs of key stakeholders.

Organisational Structure can directly affect:
- the motivation and, thus, performance of staff.
- a business's costs and profitability.
- the speed with which a business is able to respond to problems and / or changes in its environment.

The Effect of Levels of Hierarchy:

Reasons for / Purpose of Levels of Hierarchy:
- To control use of organisational resources.
- To maximise productivity, efficiency.

Other Benefits:
- Opportunities for promotion - help retain, motivate staff.

Potential Problems with Many Levels:
- Poor / slow communication.
- Slow decision-making.
- Slow response to problems / change in the environment.
- Workers feel isolated, removed from organisational goals.

Benefits of Few Levels:
- Effective / fast communication.
- Fast decision making.
- Fast response to problems / change.

NB Benefits outweighed if span of control is too wide.

Other Drawbacks of Few Levels:
- Few opportunities for promotion.

The Effect of Spans of Control:

Implications of a Wide Span:
- Enhanced motivation of subordinates – able to make decisions without interference of manager - feel more trusted, challenged.
- Minimises supervision / labour costs.

But, if too wide:
- Work overload on manager – stress, inefficiency.
- Reduced personal contact with subordinates – workers feel isolated, insufficient advice / feedback – negative effect on morale, motivation, performance.

Implications of a Narrow Span:
- High quality work / organisational effectiveness – tight control.
- Increased efficiency – managers have time to think and plan.
- Better worker / manager relationship / improved morale – managers have time to communicate, provide advice / feedback.

But, if too narrow:
- High administration / supervision costs.
- Worker resentment / low morale – due to tight control.

© APT Initiatives Ltd, 2011

The Effect of Delegation: *Delegation can…*

- reduce workload / potential stress of senior managers and free up time to concentrate on major / strategic issues.
- improve morale and motivation – employees feel valued, trusted and, possibly, more fulfilled.
- help develop better, more rounded managers.
- result in better quality, more localised decisions.
- lead to faster decisions / faster response to change.
- increase respect from first line employees - if they feel decisions do not require referral to a higher authority.
- lower supervision costs - staff more responsible, motivated.

***But,* it requires:**

- workers to be able / willing to take on extra tasks / duties.
- managers to trust in good faith and ability of staff.

Thus, it may require…

- training to ensure workers capable of taking on task(s).
- management training to change attitudes toward delegation.

Job Allocation / Work Loads:

- **Too heavy**: stress… mistakes, complaints, accidents, absenteeism, labour turnover and associated costs.
- **Too light**: unnecessarily high labour costs.

Key Reasons for Differences in Structure:

- Size of the business.
- Nature of the business activities and technology used.
- Business environment.
- Nature and expectations of workforce.
- Corporate objectives and strategy.
- Beliefs / preferences of owners / senior managers.

The Effect of Communication: *Good communication…*

ensures business objectives are met – *helping to ensure that:*

- employees are clear on their roles, tasks, responsibilities, and work towards achieving business aims / objectives.
- decisions made by management are carried through.
- potential problems are identified and discussed at an early stage, allowing timely and appropriate action to be taken as required.

is extremely relevant to employee motivation:

- Providing information about what needs to be done, how, by when, relieves anxiety - safety needs (Maslow).
- Providing information / feedback on performance - esteem needs.
- Communication requires people to interact - social needs.

is vital when planning & implementing strategy – *for example:*

- At planning stage customer research / feedback is essential in determining most appropriate strategy to implement.
- At implementation stage feedback from employees on proposals is vital in identifying potential problems.
- Communicating reasons for / potential benefits of changes in strategy can also help lessen resistance to change amongst staff.

is essential in maintaining effective relationships between a firm and external stakeholders – *for example:*

- Effective communication with suppliers ensures right materials arrive in right quantity, at right time.
- To maximise sales, customers need to be well informed about firm's product, price, promotion, etc. Two-way communication is also essential in finding out what customers want and developing / improving products / services to meet customer needs.

© APT Initiatives Ltd, 2011

MEASURING THE EFFECTIVENESS OF THE WORKFORCE

Methods of Measuring Workforce Performance

Productivity: concerns the output of a business (or division or department within a business) eg number of items produced, number of customers served in a given period of time; measured by dividing the output by the input(s), such as the output of a given amount of capital or labour. The higher the output in relation to inputs, the higher the productivity.

Labour productivity: concerns the output of a given amount of labour in a given period of time; measured by dividing output produced (volume or value), by the labour input (no. of employees, labour cost, hours worked).

Labour turnover: concerns the number of staff that leave a business in a given period of time, usually a year; normally expressed as a percentage of the average number of staff employed in the business during the year. Those leaving for unavoidable reasons such as retirement, ill health, pregnancy, marriage, etc should really be excluded from the figures to enable any human resource problems within the business to be more easily identified.

Absenteeism: concerns the inability or unwillingness of staff to turn up for work. The rate of absenteeism is calculated by dividing total number of working days lost (not worked by absent employees) in a given period of time by total number of potential working days in the trading period and multiplying the resulting figure by a hundred to give a percentage. Ideally, absenteeism for genuine reasons should be excluded from figures, to enable any human resource problems within the business to be more easily identified.

Reject rate: concerns the proportion of products arising from the production process that are found to be faulty or defective in some way. The number of rejects is usually expressed as a percentage of total products produced in a given period of time (ie number of rejects / total products produced in a trading period x 100 = X%).

Labour Productivity:

Calculation & Interpretation:

$$\frac{\text{Output (volume or value)}}{\text{Labour Input (no. of staff or hours worked, or labour cost)}}$$

Eg: 80 production staff produce 4,000 items a month. Output per worker is 50 per month (4,000 / 80).

Compare to previous years, similar firms or industry norms. The **higher** the ratio of outputs to inputs, the **better** the business is performing.

Costs / Effects:

The **higher** the productivity, the **lower** the cost – can either:

- reduce price - increase competitiveness, sales, share.
- enjoy higher profits.

Causes / Factors Influencing Productivity:

- Investment in education and training.
- Workforce morale and motivation.
- Health and age structure of workforce.
- Investment in planned, preventative maintenance.
- Quality of management

A sudden fall in productivity may not be a bad thing. Eg: Investment in new machinery may lead to a short-term drop in productivity as employees take time to get used to the machinery. In the longer term it could lead to a significant

Labour Turnover:

Calculation & Interpretation:

$$\frac{\text{No. of staff leaving per year}}{\text{Average no. of staff employed during the year}} \times 100 = X\%$$

Those leaving for unavoidable reasons eg retirement, ill health, pregnancy, marriage, etc should be excluded from figures, to enable HR problems to be more easily identified.

Compare with previous years, similar businesses / industry norms. The **higher** the % the **worse** the performance.

Costs / Effects:

- Increased overheads - recruitment costs.
- Drop in productivity while places filled, new staff learn.
- Cost of mistakes made by new inexperienced employees.
- Low morale - difficulties in maintaining teamwork.
- Management time re-organising - better utilised elsewhere.
- Drop in image to customers <u>and</u> potential employees.

Possible Causes:

- Many other job opportunities in the area.
- Pay levels below comparable local rates.
- Fluctuations in pay - irregularity of overtime, bonuses, etc.
- Irregular work - stress and / or boredom.
- Uninteresting works / monotonous repetitive tasks.
- Low morale eg due to ineffective / poor management.
- Lack of feedback / recognition, or promotion prospects.
- Poor recruitment and selection - wrong person for job.
- Poor working conditions.
- Sudden/continual change to work group, conditions, practices.
- Fear of redundancy or short time working.

Absenteeism:

Calculation & Interpretation:

$$\frac{\text{Total no. of working days lost in the period}}{\text{* Total no. of potential working days in the period}} \times 100 = X\%$$

*multiply total no. of employees planned to work by no. of working days available. Eg: For a firm open all year the total no. of working days available is 365. If the total no. of staff scheduled to work is 300, then the total no. of potential working days is 109,500 (300 x 365).

Days lost for unavoidable reasons ie genuine ill health / sickness should be excluded from the figures.

The **higher** the percentage, the **worse** the performance.

Costs / Effects:

- Loss of production and lower productivity.
- Missed deadlines - lost orders, dissatisfied customers.
- Increased labour costs - overtime, agency staff, sick pay.
- Management time organising cover and/or extending deadlines.
- Lower morale.

Possible Causes:

- Lack of interest - boring, repetitive work.
- Lack of confidence - possibly due to poor training, supervision.
- Too much work - stress and anxiety.
- Poor commitment to business goals - either due to temporary or casual labour; or failure to communicate goals and explain how employee's role fits in.
- Lack of sympathy towards time off for important personal matters, eg doctors' appointments, important family events.

Performance in Terms of Health and Safety:

Absence Arising from Poor Standards of Health & Safety – Calculation & Interpretation

Employers and employees have duties and responsibilities to ensure a healthy and safe work place. Majority of these focus on the prevention of accidents. **Accident rate:**

$$\frac{\text{Total no. of working days lost due to accidents}}{\text{Total no. of potential working days in the period}} \times 100 = X\%$$

The **higher** the percentage, the **worse** the performance.

Costs / Effects:

- Injury and distress to casualty.
- Wasted management time spent organising cover.
- Lost production / lower productivity – late delivery, dissatisfied customers / lost orders / lower revenues and profit.
- Closure by Local Authority H&S Officer (resulting in the above).
- Fines and compensation from legal action – if found in breach of duties to provide safe place of work.
- Labour turnover & associated costs - as workers feel insecure.
- Poor reputation as an employer - difficult to attract good staff.
- Poor public image - may negatively affect sales.

Possible Causes:

- Failure of employers to carry out legal duties could be due to: ignorance, or deliberate attempt to cut costs.
- Failure of employees to carry out legal duties could be due to: poor information, instruction, training and / or supervision.
- Failure of either party could stem from: low morale or motivation, pressure to meet deadlines, work overload resulting in tiredness / fatigue.

Rejects / Wastage / Complaints:

Calculation & Interpretation:

Measuring the no. of faulty goods (rejects) or waste as a proportion of all goods (or waste) produced in a given period (eg total defects / total goods produced x 100 = X%), or the level of customer satisfaction through customer satisfaction surveys.

Costs / Effects of poor quality products and / or service:

- Increased labour, material and other costs – re-working, re-testing, re-inspecting, refunds to dissatisfied customers.
- Loss of repeat business.
- Loss of business to competitors.
- Loss of sales / market share – as a result of 2 & 3 above.
- Difficulty attracting / retaining good staff.

Possible Causes:

- Failure to identify customer requirements.
- Poor quality supplies.
- Poorly maintained equipment / machinery.
- Ineffective, poorly motivated and committed staff eg due to poor recruitment, inadequate induction, training, supervision, pay, working conditions, etc.
- High stock levels – staff might not be as committed to getting quality right first time if there is plenty of stock to fall back on.
- High levels of absenteeism - workers rush, make mistakes.

There are numerous possible causes of poor performance in the above areas. To address any problem, there needs to be certainty about the exact cause. **Thorough investigations** are required to identify the exact cause and, thus, the most appropriate method(s) to address the problem.

DEVELOPING AN EFFECTIVE WORKFORCE: RECRUITMENT, SELECTION, TRAINING

The Recruitment Process

Recruitment: process of establishing the need for a new employee, the job requirements, the type of person to fit the job and attracting the most appropriate candidate.

Job description: broad statement of the nature of the job including title, purpose, tasks, targets, responsibilities and relationship to others.

Person specification: detailed description of type of person required including knowledge, skills, experience, qualifications, age, physical characteristics and type of personality.

Summary of the Stages Involved:

Job Analysis and Evaluation
Assessing the job requirements ie..
tasks (physical, intellectual), skills, duties, responsibilities.
Establishing a monetary value for the job.

↓

Production of Job Description & Person Specification
JD: Title, purpose, tasks, targets, responsibility, relationships
PS: Knowledge, skills, experience, qualifications, personal qualities and characteristics – essential or desirable.

↓

Attracting Applicants
Internally – via noticeboard, intranet, newsletter.
Externally – via word of mouth, local schools / colleges, local and national newspapers, specialist magazines, commercial employment agencies (see adjacent).

↓

Receipt of Applications
Written: by letter of application, application form, CV
Oral: by telephone.

Relative Advantages / Disadvantages of Methods to Attract External Candidates:

- **Word of mouth:** cheapest method but usually limits candidates to local people.

- **Local schools, colleges, universities:** relatively cheap but also usually limited to local people, plus only suitable for candidates under a certain age who have limited previous experience.

- **Local newspapers:** useful in recruiting in a specified area, also relatively cheap.

- **National newspapers or specialist magazines:** more costly but greater reach and wider range of applicants.

- **Local and national job centres:** free service but may also limit candidates to local area.

- **Commercial employment agencies:** used for skilled and managerial posts / particular jobs or professions eg secretarial, computing, accounting, teaching. Often carry out full selection procedures, saving employers a considerable amount of time short-listing and selecting candidates. In return, employers pay a fee. But, may still prove cheaper than national advertising.

Internal and External Recruitment

Internal recruitment: attracting applicants for a post from *within* the business.
External recruitment: attracting applicants for a post from *outside* the business.

Internal Recruitment:

Potential Benefits:

- Reduced risk of employing the wrong person - employees (strengths, weaknesses) already known.
- Faster recruitment & selection - less applicants to screen.
- Less expensive - avoids cost of advertising, telephone calls, time chasing applicants.
- Shorter induction - employee already familiar with business.
- Increased retention / motivation of staff - chance of promotion may encourage staff to stay and work hard.

Potential Drawbacks:

- Limited choice - if not used in conjunction with external.
- Lost opportunity to bring in fresh perspective.
- Creates a vacancy down the hierarchy.
- Possible de-motivation of internal candidate(s) not selected.
- Potential difficulty for employee promoted internally to manage people he / she previously worked alongside.
- Possible training and development costs - to provide recruit with the necessary skills and experience.

External Recruitment:

Potential Benefits:

- Greater choice.
- Brings in fresh perspective - can be motivating for others who have worked there for several years.
- May bring in expertise from other firms - especially useful if change is required / desired.
- Does not create a vacancy elsewhere.
- Potentially lower training costs.

Potential Drawbacks:

- Greater risk - no proven track record with the business.
- Slower recruitment & selection - more applicants to screen.
- More expensive - often involves advertising, plus usually more applicants to screen <u>and</u> contact.
- Longer induction - recruit unfamiliar with the business.
- Problems in gaining support of existing staff – completely new recruit may not be readily accepted by others, especially if existing, internal employee hoped to get the job.

Whether internal or external recruitment is chosen will very much depend upon:

- whether or not there are staff of the calibre required for the post internally.
- whether or not the business wants to bring in fresh ideas and experience from outside the business.
- the budget available – external recruitment generally tends to be more expensive than internal recruitment.
- the effect the decision will have on the morale and motivation of existing staff.

Selecting the Best Employees

Shortlisting: involves screening job applicants to identify a smaller number for further assessment; often involves examination of written applications (curriculum vitaes, standard application forms, letters of application) to eliminate applicants who fail to meet selection criteria and identify applicants who meet it most closely and are worthy of further consideration.

Selection: involves assessment of candidates' suitability for a job and the appointment of the most appropriate candidate.

References: oral or written comments on suitability of candidate for post, made by individuals nominated by candidate, usually past and / or present employers, work colleagues, and personal acquaintances.

Job interview: an appropriate person or panel of people, ask potential job candidates a series of questions, usually face to face.

Behavioural job interviews: involve questions designed to obtain examples of candidates' previous behaviour.

Structured job interviews: involve use of pre-determined questions based on selection criteria for the post.

Unstructured job interviews: do not involve use of pre-determined questions. Interviewer can ask whatever questions he / she feels will help determine suitability of candidate for the job.

Cognitive ability tests: measure intellectual skills and abilities, eg problem solving, critical thinking, verbal and numerical reasoning.

Personality tests: ask a series of questions which attempt to identify personality types.

Psychometric tests: measure aspects of a person's skills, abilities and personality, including cognitive abilities and personality traits.

Work-sample tests: measure candidate's ability to undertake work-related tasks relevant to the job for which they are applying.

Assessment centre: place where a range of assessment methods are used to assess capabilities of applicants for a particular post relative to selection criteria for the post, in order to determine suitability, and help make appropriate selection decisions.

Shortlisting Applicants:

Might involve use of tests and group interviews, but most common method involves:

1. examining written applications (CV's, application forms, letters)
2. eliminating candidates who do not meet basic selection criteria, and / or selecting those that most closely match.

Arguably the **most important** part of the R&S process.
Can be the **most time consuming**.

Requesting References:

- Candidates worthy of further consideration usually have references taken up before attending interview / testing.
- Often take the form of a written statement or questionnaire, but can also be conducted by phone.
- Referees are usually provided with information about the post and asked to comment on candidate's suitability.
- May also be asked to verify / comment on claims made by candidates in their application or interview.

© **APT Initiatives Ltd**, 2011

Interviews: Most common method.

- Allows two-way exchange.
- Relatively cheap way to gain insight into candidate's suitability.

However…

- Some people perform well at interview but may not be able to perform well in a work-related task. *Thus…*
- On their own, not always the most reliable method, particularly if time is limited and / or candidate is nervous.
- Success relies on skill of interviewer.

Strengths / weaknesses of different types:

- Behavioural - past behaviour can be good indicator of likely behaviour / ability to perform in the future.
- Structured - provides scope to score and compare candidates.
- Unstructured - difficult to compare candidates, but may obtain important info that would not have been obtained through pre-set Q's.

Tests: *Depend on job to be carried out. The first 3 below are developed by psychologists and are usually standardised written tests scored and compared against established norms.*

- **Cognitive Ability / Aptitude & Intelligence:** can generate highly valid results and ensure consistency in interpretation, but are time consuming and costly to administer.
- **Personality:** when personality vital eg sales, customer service.
- **Psychometric:** measure skills, abilities and personality incl. cognitive abilities, personality traits.
- **Work-sample:** test practical elements of job eg for secretarial post include word-processing test, for teacher, trainer, sales executive include making a presentation. Highly valid results.
- **Medical / Health:** where physical fitness is important eg firemen, police, armed forces.

Assessment Centres:

Typically involve **wide range** of oral, written and, sometimes, physical tasks, including: psychometric tests, interviews, workplace simulations, work-sample tests, group exercises / discussions. Candidates are observed and rated by a team of assessors, often over a period of **more than one day**. *Can be…*

- highly effective in predicting likely performance / determining suitability - variety of techniques provides more rounded view / increases validity. *But…*
- time consuming, costly to organise and administer - require assessors with considerable expertise / experience in observation, recording, interpretation, evaluation of behaviour. *Thus…*
- use often limited to strategically important jobs - senior / managerial appointments.

Key Factors Affecting Recruitment & Selection Decisions:

Time and cost.

Business must balance time and cost involved with the need to attract a high quality applicant. Often the more senior the post, the higher the cost.

How Recruitment and Selection Can Improve a Workforce

Appointing the right person (capable, motivated, committed) can improve performance – It should help to: **minimise the occurrence of defective goods / poor service; maximise labour productivity; minimise absenteeism, labour turnover and associated costs.** Recruitment and selection can be time consuming and expensive making it all the more important to get the right person first time. External recruitment can also bring in new knowledge, skills, experience and invigorating ideas from which the business can benefit.

© **APT Initiatives Ltd**, 2011

Methods of Training

Training: the process of developing knowledge, skills and attitudes required for a member of staff to competently and confidently carry out a job.

Induction: the process of familiarising a new 'recruit' with the workplace.

On-the-job training: where employees are taught how to carry out their jobs in the actual place of work, and usually during normal working hours.

Off-the-job training: where employees are taught how to do their job away from their usual place of work. This may involve sending employees away to attend courses related to their work, at a college of further or higher education, but it can also take place in specialist training areas or establishments within the business.

Main Aim, Role & Purpose of Training in General:

- To develop the knowledge, skills, attitudes required to competently and confidently carry out a job.

Reasons / Benefits for Employer	Reasons / Benefits for Employee
Training costs money and can lead to drop in productivity whilst new staff are trained. *However,* it can help to: - **maximise output** from a given capacity - minimising unit labour costs. - **minimise poor quality work** / service and associated costs. - **minimise the chance of accidents** and associated costs. - **reduce the number of supervisors** required, thus the cost of supervision. - **minimise labour turnover** & associated costs - staff likely to be more motivated. - **create a more flexible workforce** - as workers are able to fill in for each other. - **attract good quality staff** - aiding recruitment. Training is essential in **maximising efficiency, safety** and **profits.** Adequate health and safety is also **a legal requirement**.	Employees may be more satisfied and motivated, as they may: - feel **more confident, secure** - safety needs. - feel **valued** - management willing to invest in them - esteem needs. - be able to undertake **more interesting / challenging work** that enables them to use more of their abilities, improves job prospects and chance of promotion - self-actualisation needs.

Induction:

Importance	Possible Components	Possible Methods
• Helps recruits settle in as quickly as possible with minimum disruption. • Reduces anxiety / risk of leaving. • Complies with Health & Safety legislation.	• Nature of the firm, its activities, aims, objectives. • How employee's job contributes to its success – responsibilities and position within the business. • Layout of premises - key facilities. • Key individuals, work colleagues. • Health, safety, security policies & procedures. • Other aspects of contract of employment eg hours, breaks, holiday, disciplinary / grievance.	• **Talks** on history to present day, rules & regulations. • **Written documents** eg health & safety. • **Videos** to demonstrate products. • **Visits / tours** to see key parts of premises, meet key personnel. • **Group discussions** – for recruits to meet and discuss / air any concerns.

On-the Job Training:

Methods;

- **Sitting next to Nellie:** experienced employee shows trainee.
- **Coaching:** expert demonstrates and guides trainee.
- **Mentoring:** trainee carries out job, discusses problems / solutions with experienced individual assigned to give them advice as required.

Benefits:

- Job specific and directly linked to the firm's needs.
- More easily adapted.
- Relatively easy to organise and relatively inexpensive.
- No loss in output – trainee not removed from production.

Drawbacks:

- Drop in productivity.
- Risk of bad practice being passed on.
- Workplace distractions - stressful, take longer.

Off-the-Job Training:

Methods:

- **Lectures:** economical but limited audience participation.
- **Demonstrations:** greater impact than lecture - visual and oral.
- **Simulations, role plays:** build confidence, difficult to transfer.
- **Self study:** trainee controls timing, not as easy to access help.

Benefits:

- Quality may be higher – provided by specialists. *Thus, maybe…*
- …more highly valued, with trainees more committed to learn.
- Trainees more able to work at own speed – less stressful.
- Work-place distractions avoided – easier to concentrate.
- *Thus*…Learning outcomes may be better and may take less time.
- *Plus*…If meet staff from other business – useful insight.

Drawbacks:

- **Can be very expensive** in comparison to on-the-job.
- **Lower productivity** – trainee not involved in production. *However…* avoids costly errors/ mistakes from trainees learning on-the-job.

DEVELOPING & RETAINING AN EFFECTIVE WORKFORCE: MOTIVATING EMPLOYEES

Motivation – An Introduction

Motivation: the driving force or process which compels people to choose a particular course of action.

Why Study Motivation?

The Importance of People:

A business is only as good as the people it employs. People have feelings and emotions that influence their behaviour and the way they respond to a situation. To get the best out of people / ensure employees behave in a way consistent with organisational objectives, these feelings and emotions must be considered.

Symptoms & Consequences of a Poorly Motivated Workforce

Symptoms	Consequences
• Lateness, absence, labour turnover. • Poor quality and/or low output of work. • Unwillingness to take responsibility. • Quarrels with colleagues. • Disputes with management. • Accidents. • Damage to equipment or property.	• increased costs. • loss of sales. • reduced profits. due to: • waste. • inefficiency.

Benefits of a Well-motivated Workforce:

- Higher productivity - reduced labour cost per unit.
- Improved quality and enhanced reputation.
- Lower labour turnover & associated costs.
- Lower absenteeism and improved punctuality.
- Greater willingness to contribute ideas.
- Greater desire to take on responsibility - less supervision.
- Greater willingness to accept change / adapt.

What Motivates a Human?

Basic Assumptions:

- All behaviour has a **cause** - a consequence of the environment.
- At the route of behaviour are **needs** or **wants**.
- Behaviour is **goal-seeking** - achieve goals to satisfy needs.
- needs can be **primary** - physiological, genetic eg food, water; **secondary** - socio-psychological, learned eg the need for love and belonging, esteem, achievement and power.
- Individual **perception** is vital - a person has a need when they *perceive* a physiological or psychological deficiency. They then focus on a goal - anything that is *perceived* to satisfy that need.

Why People Work: *To…*

- earn money for food, water - satisfy need to survive. *Also to…*
- provide meaning and structure to the day.
- socialise / interact – satisfy need to feel loved / part of a group.
- use / develop knowledge / skill – need for achievement.

People's Needs are Different and May Change:

Different cultural backgrounds, physical and intellectual differences, influence our behaviour, needs, and *perception* of what will satisfy these. Needs may also differ according to our stage in life, or the situation we face. Eg: An 18 yr old school leaver may be more interested in earning money to rent his / her own flat; a 40 yr old manager, who has worked in the same position for 10 yrs, already owns his / her own house, may want a more challenging job and may be willing to take a drop in salary to secure this.

© APT Initiatives Ltd, 2011

Theories of Motivation

Classical theories: examine the nature of work carried out and apply scientific principles to the process of management.
Human relations and content theories: consider people's needs rather than the job or work being done.
Process theories: analyse how employees make decisions and their thinking behind these decisions.

Taylor's Scientific Approach to Management (1856-1917):

The application of scientific principles to the process of management.

- Observing workers, recording and timing tasks (work study).
- Identifying the most efficient – establishing quickest / best way.
- High division of labour and specialisation.
- Designing equipment to increase speed tasks completed.
- Strict instructions to workers.
- Close supervision.
- Piecework pay / differential piece rate.

Work measurement and **piece rate** - valuable today in maximising efficiency and effectiveness. *Main criticisms:*

- **Treating workers like machines - repetitive, monotonous tasks.**
- **Assuming the only reason people work is for money.**

Mayo's Hawthorne Experiments / Hawthorne Effect:

Hawthorne plant, Western Electric Co., Chicago (1927-1932) - investigated relationship between working conditions and output. Identified and recognised the importance of…

- **social relationships, communication** and **interest / attention shown by management (the Hawthorne effect)** in motivating workers – more important than working conditions.

- **informal groups over attitudes and performance** and of **group incentives** to provide workers with sense of belonging.

Led to:
- social events being organised after work.
- personnel departments in companies throughout America & Britain (1930-50's) to try to achieve 'the Hawthorne Effect'.

Maslow's Hierarchy of Needs:
(Investigations between 1939-43). At any 1 time 1 need dominant - motivator - individual acts to satisfy need. Once satisfied, moves on to next set. *Criticisms / difficulties in terms of application to the workplace:*

- Humans have innate + environmental differences, thus not have same needs.
- Humans have different degrees of need eg some not ambitious, thus motivators targeting esteem and self-actualisation not likely to affect performance.
- Needs not necessarily satisfied in order suggested, eg highly creative people may be motivated by higher order needs even if lower order not fulfilled.
- Needs may be satisfied outside work eg esteem through success in sports. Thus, motivators aimed at fulfilling this in the workplace may be unnecessary / wasteful.

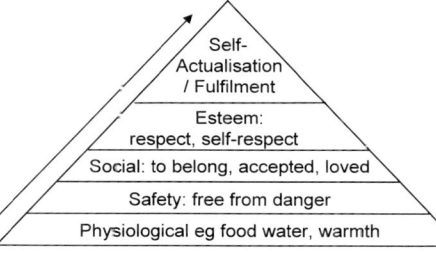

McGregor's Theory X and Y: (1960's)

Theory X: People...	Theory Y: People...
are lazy, dislike work, try to avoid it.	want to learn, work is natural to them, do not dislike it.
must be coerced and controlled to work hard.	can exercise self control, direction, feel rewarded by achievements, work towards organisational goals rather than financial incentives.
avoid responsibility, prefer direction.	learn to accept and seek responsibility.
are not ambitious, take no initiative, need security.	can solve problems, are ambitious, seek to realise potential.
Linked to...Taylor – money motivator, supervise / control.	*Linked to...Human relations, higher order needs.*
Requires formal structure, authoritarian management.	*Requires more democratic approach.*

Motivational problems arise when staff who require and expect Theory Y receive Theory X approaches, and vice versa.

Vroom and Value-Expectancy Theory:

Assumes people act in rational, logical way but highlights differences between individuals + how individual goals influence performance:

Force (motivation) = Valence x Expectancy

- **Force** = strength of urge to act / behave in particular way.
- **Valence** = perceived attractiveness / value of the outcome.
- **Expectancy** = perceived likelihood that outcome will be achieved.

Based on individual's *perception* of reality. **V** differs between individuals & over time. **E** depends on behaviour of organisation + experience or prejudices of individual. Thus, **high V + low E** will **not produce high M**. Managers must analyse motives of staff, provide them with realistic goals + rewards the individual (not manager) sees as important.

Herzberg's Two Factor Theory: (1950's)

Motivators	Hygiene
Achievement	Company policies, admin
Recognition for achievement	Supervision
Meaningful, interesting work	Working conditions
Responsibility	Interpersonal relations
Personal growth, advancement	Salary / pay, status, security
Link: Maslow's higher order needs	*Link:* Maslow's lower order
If present in a job encourage employees to work harder, give job satisfaction.	Prevent dissatisfaction & drop in output, but do not persuade employees to work harder.

Many question **money** as hygiene factor. Herzberg's highlighted psychological growth in providing long-term job satisfaction, and attention to the **design of jobs** which can provide such growth.

Adams' Equity Theory: (1963) Motivation can be reflection of extent to which employee perceives him / herself to be fairly treated

- **Fair treatment** in terms of what employees get from work (outputs), in relation to what they put into work (inputs).
- **Outputs** eg pay, job security, benefits, recognition, praise, power, status, reputation and promotion, etc.
- **Inputs** eg time, effort, experience, skills, loyalty, flexibility, tolerance, enthusiasm, respect for boss, support of others, etc.
- **Individuals assign values to outputs** eg flexible hours might be more important to working mother than high pay, promotion.
- What employees perceive as fair is based on **comparisons with the inputs and outputs of significant (or 'referent') others** - in similar positions within the business or other businesses.
- If perceive treatment to be **fair** ie their inputs = outputs - content & **motivated**. If inputs greater than outputs - **demotivated**.
- **Individuals will respond in different ways** to perceived 'imbalance' eg reduce work effort, be openly disruptive, leave.

Using Financial Methods to Motivate Employees

Time based payment systems: payment according to the amount of time spent at work, as opposed to output or performance.

Merit based payment systems (payment by results): pay according to quantity and / or quality of work, as opposed to time spent at work.

Wages: monies earned by employees in return for their labour or services rendered on an hourly, daily, or weekly basis.

Salary: annual amount paid to employees (normally to supervisory, clerical, managerial workers) for work undertaken. Paid monthly, in 12 equal instalments, not related to output, profits or hours of work, although rates are usually fixed in relation to standard number of hours worked per week, written into an employee's contract of employment.

Piece rate pay: where workers are paid for each quality item produced.

Performance-related pay: where part of an employee's pay is linked to achievement of pre-defined (and agreed) targets.

Profit share: an extension of group payment by results scheme, where employees receive a bonus based on business profits.

Share ownership (and share option) schemes: provide employees with the opportunity to be part owners (shareholders) of the company in which they work and, thus, to receive a variable dividend (a percentage of after-tax profits) according to how well the company has done, and voting rights on important matters (such as the election of directors).

Fringe benefits: benefits provided to employees in addition to pay eg company car, fitness club membership, subsidised health care, discounts on firm's products. The large majority have a financial value.

Time Based Pay – Wages & Salaries:

Advantages	Disadvantages	Appropriateness
• Employees have guaranteed income - safety needs, hygiene factor. • Total wage bill for year known - aids budgeting, forecasting, decisions. • Quality more likely than output based pay.	• Little incentive to work hard. • Supervisors more likely to be required. • Staff who work harder than others may resent being paid the same as those that don't (equity theory).	• **Most** appropriate when difficult to measure output or performance; quality matters rather than quantity. • **Least** appropriate when significant changes in demand.

Merit Based Pay – Piece Rate

Advantages	Disadvantages	Appropriateness
• Increased incentive to work hard. • Less supervision required *but…* • Group schemes may encourage teamwork, minimise conflict.	• Staff no basic pay if encounter problems outside their control eg machine breakdowns, late delivery of supplies - resentment, insecurity. • Supervision may be needed to ensure quality, safety. • Group schemes perceived unfair if some members put in less effort.	Where individual or group output can easily be measured.

Merit Based Pay – Performance Related Pay

Advantages	Disadvantages	Appropriateness
• Opportunity to earn more money may increase staff motivation, performance • Can help align personal with organisational goals – targets linked to business objectives. • Less supervision may be required.	• Rewards individuals, does little to promote teamwork. • Can cause unhealthy rivalry. • Can damage relationships, team spirit. Important for such systems to be transparent and fair and that the criteria for assessment is clearly understood and agreed.	when performance cannot be assessed easily through numerical measures

Financial Incentive Schemes – Profit Share:

Potential Benefits	Potential Drawbacks
encourage employees to: • put forward cost saving, revenue generating ideas. • work collectively, be more cooperative. • increase work effort. • be less resistant to change. • remain loyal - minimising labour turnover. may help attract good staff - aid recruitment.	• Reduced profits for re-investment, distribution to shareholders. • Profit is dependent on activities of others + factors beyond control of individual employee - thus may not motivate. • Schemes are unrelated to individual effort - can cause dispute if individuals feel work harder than others but all get same share. • If annual payment - time gap between performance and share. • Only motivating if profit awarded is a worthwhile sum of money. • Profit figures can be manipulated by window dressing.

Financial Incentive Schemes – Share ownership:

Potential Benefits	Drawbacks / Limitations
may encourage employees to: • work collectively. • increase work effort. • remain loyal. • be less resistant to change. *may* help attract good staff – aiding recruitment.	For current owners / shareholders divorce of ownership & control. *In practice…* • Managers and staff often sell shares at first opportunity. • Unlikely staff secure sufficient shares to influence decisions.

Fringe Benefits:

May include profit share, share option schemes, but also many other privileges, facilities, services provided by employer eg pension, holidays, company car, subsidised canteen, gym membership or dental care, flexible working, discounts on products.

Add to cost of employing labour but may:

- help attract good staff - may prefer some benefits over pay eg medical insurance.
- help keep staff loyal - reduce turnover.
- be cheaper than higher pay - NI does not have to be paid.

Cash Bonus Payments: recognition for effort (esteem needs, Herzberg's motivator). May lead to short-term increase in motivation or loyalty. But, employee may see regular (eg Christmas) bonuses as his / her 'right'. In which case - may have no motivational effect at all.

Financial incentives are only likely to motivate and provide benefits, if they are:

- fair and seen to be fair.
- transparent.
- understood by those involved.
- free of manipulation.
- significant / worth striving for.
- as timely as possible.
- based on realistic, achievable criteria.
- directly related to responsibilities and performance of those involved

Improving Job Design

Job enrichment: involves providing employees with more challenging tasks and / or greater responsibility and, ultimately, opportunities to demonstrate their abilities.

Job enlargement: involves providing employees with more tasks of the same or similar nature.

Job rotation: involves providing employees with job variety by changing their job or tasks at various intervals.

Job Enrichment:

Greater responsibility, more meaningful, interesting work may:

- help motivate staff (Herzberg's motivators).
- enable staff to fulfil their potential, enhance job prospects (self-actualisation needs, Maslow).

Job enrichment may, therefore:

- encourage employees to work harder, give rise to greater job satisfaction.
- help minimise labour turnover & associated costs - as a result of greater job satisfaction.
- help minimise supervision costs, overcome coordination problems from wide span of control (as employees become more responsible).

However, it may not suit all workers - some may not be willing or have the ability to take on extra responsibilities. Potential disadvantages:

- Training costs.
- Demands for increased pay / union disputes.
- Drop in productivity due to lack of specialisation.

Job Enlargement:

Providing some variation of tasks may:

- reduce boredom, provide more interesting work (Herzberg's motivators), thus increase satisfaction and productivity.
- lead to a more flexible workforce, efficient organisation - as workers are more able to fill in for absent colleagues.

May require less training than enrichment.

However, it may:

- not motivate those who would prefer extra responsibility rather than more tasks of similar nature.

Like enrichment it may also:

- lead to claims for additional pay.
- result in a drop in productivity – as employees find it hard to concentrate on several tasks rather than one, or find it hard to switch between tasks.

Job Rotation: *May...*

- provide similar advantages / disadvantages of job enlargement.
- also lead to drop in productivity due to less specialisation.

All 3 may:

- improve job satisfaction, motivation and retention of staff. For some, greater variety more important than more pay.
- provide employees with greater insight into range of activities carried out within the business, thus more able to fill in for absent colleagues (helping to maximise productivity, ensure targets/schedules met), plus more able to put forward valuable ideas on how to improve the business.

Empowering Employees

Empowerment: giving employees authority to make decisions or control their own activities.

Requirements: Recognition employees are capable of doing more; trust; making employees feel confident.
Potential Barriers: Willingness of managers to delegate; ability / willingness of employees to take on more responsibility.

Potential Benefits:
- Employees feel more trusted, valued (esteem needs, Maslow) thus, more motivated.
- Employees get increased job satisfaction (responsibility, Herzberg's 'Motivators'), thus, more motivated. May also be able to use more abilities/potential (Maslow's self-actualisation needs).
- Managers freed up to concentrate on planning, organisational development.
- Employees feel less stressed - less supervision, interference - minimising absenteeism.
- Lower costs - from less supervision, absenteeism.
- Potentially better quality and faster decisions and, thus, faster response to change.

Potential Drawbacks:
- Training - staff and managers.
- Employees may demand more pay.

Longer-term:
- Recruitment & selection policies might need adapting to ensure that individuals are selected who fit in with 'empowered' culture.

Working in Teams

A team: a group of individuals selected to work together within an organisation in order to complete a given task, specific group of tasks, or undertake a specific project.

Potential Benefits:
- People can draw upon knowledge, skills, opinions, viewpoints of others - resulting in better quality decision-making.
- People may be more willing to innovate, take risks as responsibility is shared - enabling faster response to change.
- Less disruption from absenteeism - as team members are generally encouraged to learn / perform other members' jobs.
- Teamwork can help to satisfy people's social and emotional needs and, thus, aid motivation / job satisfaction (Mayo, Herzberg).

Potential Drawbacks: Greater scope for conflict.

Links between Organisational Structure & Motivational Techniques Available

Eg 1: The Scope & Limitations of Few Levels of Hierarchy with Wide Spans of Control
Flatter structures with wide spans of control - greater scope for **delegation**, resulting in the use of **job enrichment** and **empowerment**. Wide spans of control, less supervision - may be greater need for financial and other incentives to keep staff motivated on task at hand.

Eg 2: The Scope & Limitations of Many Levels of Hierarchy with Narrow Spans of Control
Tall structures, narrow spans of control - **scope for job enrichment and empowerment may be limited**, use may be made of **job rotation**. Narrow spans of control, close supervision - may be less need for financial and other incentives to keep staff motivated on task at hand.

© APT Initiatives Ltd, 2011

OPERATIONS MANAGEMENT

MAKING OPERATIONAL DECISIONS

Operational Targets

Operational targets: goals that must be achieved by the operations function in order to achieve the business's corporate objectives.

Unit cost: the average cost per unit of output; calculated by dividing total costs with the level of output (eg no. of items produced). Total costs are made up of variable costs (eg materials, energy) and fixed costs (eg rent, interest payments on loans).

Quality: providing the customer with a product or service that meets their needs / expectations on a consistent basis.

Capacity: the maximum level of output a business can produce within a particular period eg week, month, quarter, year, with its present resources, eg premises, plant, machinery, equipment, labour.

Capacity utilisation: a measure of the extent to which a firm's capacity (in terms of labour, machinery, etc) is being used.

Unit Costs: *Calculation and Interpretation:*

Example: Fixed costs £350,000. Variable costs £450,000. Output 200,000 units.

Unit cost = $\frac{\text{Total costs (Fixed + Variable)}}{\text{Output}} = \frac{£800,000 (£350 + £450)}{200,000}$ = **£4.00**

With output slightly more or less than 200,000, unit cost might be very different - as FC do not change (in short run) with level of output. As output rises, FC are divided over larger volume of output, which lowers unit costs…

How FC per unit reduces the more produced and sold:
- 200,000 items produced and sold, FC per unit = £1.75 (£350,000 / 200,000).
- 250,000 items a month, then FC per unit = £1.40.
- 400,000 items a month, FC per unit = £1.17.

How FC per unit increases the less produced and sold:
- Only sell 150,000 items a month, then FC per unit = £2.33 (£350,000 / 150,000).
- Only sell 100,000 items a month, FC per unit = £3.00.

Most efficient level of output is where unit cost lowest. The **lower** the unit cost:
- the more **efficient** (productive) the production process.
- the more **profitable**, or more competitive a business can be on **price**.

(However, a reduction in unit costs should not be at the expense safety or quality).

Quality: *Targets might concern…*
- reducing no. of faulty products occurring in production process.
- improving reliability eg delivery times.
- reducing customer complaints.
- increasing customer satisfaction levels.

…by a certain amount, in a given period.

Volume / Output: *Targets might concern…*
- producing certain no. of items in given period.
- serving certain no. of customers in given period.
- achieving certain % growth in either of above - to increase capacity utilisation (CU), or achieve sales growth objectives.

Maximising volume and CU minimises FC per unit.

© APT Initiatives Ltd, 2011

Calculating and Managing capacity Utilisation

Capacity: the maximum level of output a business can produce with its present resources, eg premises, plant, machinery, equipment, labour within a particular period eg week, month, quarter, year,

Capacity utilisation: a measure of the extent to which a firm's capacity (in terms of labour, machinery, etc) is being used; expressed as a percentage and calculated by dividing actual output into maximum possible output in a given period, and multiplying by 100.

Calculating Capacity Utilisation (CU):

Business able to produce 5,000 units a month.

Only produces 4,000 units a month.

CU rate = **80%** (4,000 / 5,000 x 100).

= 20% spare capacity (1,000 / 5,000 x 100).

Low CU – Benefits & Potential Problems:

Potential Problems	Benefits
• FC spread over lower output, *thus* higher unit costs, lower profit / profit margins or less price competitiveness, *thus* lower demand, lost sales. • Worker boredom, problems with morale and motivation if paid piece rate or fear jobs insecure, *resulting in* labour turnover and associated costs. • Negative public image, *resulting in* reduced demand, lost sales. • Cash flow problems.	• Scope for error. • Scope for growth. • Less pressure. • More time for training, routine cleaning and maintenance.

High CU – Benefits & Potential Problems:

Benefits	Potential Problems
• Resources fully utilised, FC spread over higher output, *resulting in* lower unit costs, higher margins or more price competitiveness, *thus* higher demand, sales. • Less time for workers to feel bored, or insecure. • Positive (popular) image, *resulting in* increased demand, sales growth.	• Less time for routine maintenance, cleaning. • Less scope for error. • Less room for new orders. • Less time for training. • Extra pressure on staff – negative effect on morale, motivation, *resulting in* mistakes, accidents and associated costs.

Possible Reasons for Low CU:

Demand-side Explanations	Supply-side Explanations
Poor forecasts of demand *due to...* • ineffective marketing. • competitor activities. • changes affecting disposable income eg interest / tax rates. • seasonal nature of product.	• Unexpected breakdowns. • Shortage of inventories. • Restrictive working practices eg strikes. • Staff mistakes / errors. • Staff absence. *...from internal weakness or external factors.*

Managing Capacity:

Short-term Measures	Long-term
High CU: Overtime, temporary staff, equipment hire, shift work, subcontract out, raise price.	**High CU:** Invest in fixed capacity increase.
Low CU: Reduce working hours, subcontract in, stimulate demand eg advertising, special offers.	**Low CU:** Rationalise, diversify.

Operational Issues: Dealing with Non Standard Orders, Matching Production & Demand

Non-standard orders: orders for products or services that differ in some way to the usual product or service provided by the business.

Contribution: the difference between total revenue and total direct (or variable) costs.

Demand: the quantity that customers are willing and able to purchase at a particular price, over a given period.

Overtime: involves employees working in excess of their contracted / agreed hours; often used to meet short-term increases in demand eg at peak times of the year, and often paid at a higher rate.

Core and periphery workforce: the use of a core of permanent, full-time workers and a periphery of temporary, part-time workers in order to provide the flexibility required to cope with variations in demand. The core workers generally fill important roles ie roles considered essential to the firm's competitive advantage, and tend to be more trained and skilled. The periphery workers may not be as skilled or well trained, or may be skilled workers brought in for a specific purpose.

Part-time staff: staff contracted to work for a business for less than a standard 35 to 40 hours per week.

Temporary staff: staff contracted to work for a business for a short period, usually under a year.

Shift work: where an employee replaces another employee on the same job within a 24-hour period.

Annual hours contracts: where employees work a certain number of hours each year. Hours worked each week will vary throughout the year according to the needs of the business.

Zero hours contracts: where employees are available for work as and when required and there are no set hours or times.

Subcontracting: where one business contracts another business to produce or provide some or all of its products / services to customers.

Rationalisation: involves selling off, or closing down parts of a business that are in decline, in order to concentrate on core activities in which the business has some competitive advantage.

Stocks: consist of raw materials and components, work in progress, or finished goods.

Dealing with Non-standard (Special) Orders: *Issues to consider…*

1. Does the business have **sufficient capacity**? 2. Does it have the **necessary skills / experience**? 3. Will **different stocks** be required? Can these be obtained at the right price? 4. Will **additional fixed costs** eg design costs be incurred? 5. Is the **likely contribution** worthwhile? 6. What will be the **effect on existing operations** eg will it prevent other, more profitable orders being met? 7. Could the order **lead to other, more profitable orders** in the future?	*If regularly undertake non-standard orders in house…* Workers, machinery, organisation must be **flexible** to ensure individual orders and short production runs can be dealt with. *Potential benefits:* • **Financial gains** from higher capacity utilisation. • **Greater job satisfaction** from greater job variety (Herzberg's motivators).

Matching Production and Demand:

Matching production and demand is a regular concern for **seasonal** products / services. Solution if the product is…

…**not perishable** - produce at steady rate over the year, store goods to meet seasonal peak - ensures high CU, but stockholding costs.
…**perishable** (thus not capable of being stored) - consider the following…

Overtime:

- Can increase unit costs as often paid at higher rate. *But…*
- can be cheaper + more flexible than temporary staff in short-term, which involves recruitment and admin. *However…*
- excessive, long-term use can lead to fatigue, stress, accidents, absence. *Plus…*
- staff may work slowly to secure overtime - inefficiency, increased costs.
- staff may come to depend on overtime as extra pay and conflict can arise if overtime opportunities are withdrawn.

Temporary & Part-time Staff:

Increases flexibility to meet fluctuations in demand and help maximise capacity utilisation. *However…*

- may prove more costly than overtime - extra recruitment (unless agency staff used), induction / training, administration.
- can be less motivated and committed than permanent, full time staff.

Shift Work:

- Can help maximise output produced from current premises, machinery ie capacity utilisation. *But…*
- can increase labour costs - if employees paid premium rate for 'unsociable' hours, or extra supervision required to operate shift. *However…*
- can reduce unit costs overall - due to greater capital utilisation + 'off-peak' utility charges.

Annual Hours and Zero Hours Contracts:

Flexibility to meet fluctuating demand, maximise productivity, minimise labour costs.

However, with annualised hours contracts…

- Difficult to accurately predict hours, especially if firm takes on non-standard orders.
- Overtime may still be required - in the case of hard to predict increases in demand.
- If serious (unpredicted) downturn in demand - paying for hours not used.
- Keeping track of hours worked - can also be problematic.

Potential disadvantages for employees - *It could lead to:*

- loss of (overtime) earnings.
- long hours at times, few at others - difficult to plan, balance home / work life. NB overtime optional, annual hours makes long working hours involuntary.

Subcontracting work out: *May be...*

- more economical than securing extra equipment, skills required to meet peaks in demand.
- the only option if space for extra staff / machinery is limited.
- considered to fulfil non-standard orders - if lack specialist knowledge, equipment required.

However...

- a suitable subcontractor may not be found.
- less control over quality.
- lower profit margins.
- threat of increased competition.
- requires rigorous selection, strict specifications.

Subcontract work in to utilise spare capacity: *May...*

- reduce fixed costs per unit, ensure workforce fully employed.
- provide inside information about the competition.

However...

- less able to cope with fluctuations in demand. *Thus...* use on short-term / temporary basis, build flexibility into contract.

Rationalisation: *Might involve...*

- moving to smaller premises.
- closing down unit in particular location.
- selling off surplus machinery, equipment.
- downsizing (reducing no. of staff).
- delayering (removing layer of management).

Can reduce overheads, increase capacity utilisation. *But,* may involve redundancies, thus, redundancy pay and feelings of insecurity amongst staff who remain. This can lead to poor morale and motivation, and negatively affect productivity.

The Importance of Managing Stocks Efficiently:

Need to balance cost of holding stock against cost of running out...

Costs of Holding Stocks	Costs of Stockout
• Cost of storage.	• Inability to meet demand.
• Cost of finance.	• Loss of goodwill – lost income.
• Risk of theft, damage, deterioration, obsolescence.	• Longer lead time – less competitive, or increased costs (late delivery penalties).
• Opportunity cost.	

Many businesses moved to **'just in time'** production with stock arriving just in time to use in production process - dependent upon:

- careful planning including accurate sales forecasting.
- flexible, reliable suppliers.
- reliable machinery.
- staff with right ability, motivation to ensure quality right first time.

Minimises cost of holding stocks but may result in:

- losing out on bulk-buying discounts.
- greater administration / ordering and handling costs.

Q: Does reduction in stockholding and waste from pressure to get quality right first time, outweigh lost discount + extra ordering + handling costs?

Overall, optimum stockholding involves taking into account:

- Customer demand / rate of usage.
- Lead time for obtaining supplies and reliability of supplier(s).
- Purchasing economies (discounts for bulk orders).
- Shelf life of product and cost of wastage and deterioration.
- Storage capacity.
- Stockholding costs.
- Cost of running out.
- Stock ordering costs.
- Transport and handling costs.

DEVELOPING EFFECTIVE OPERATIONS: QUALITY

The Meaning and Importance of Quality

Quality: providing the customer with a product or service that meets their requirements on a consistent basis.

The Meaning of Quality:

Doing the right thing in the eyes of the customer, and doing it right first time – consistently meeting customer specifications.

Depends on customers' needs, expectations, perceptions – customers determine quality, management and workforce deliver.

The Importance of Quality:

- **Customer satisfaction / sales maximisation** – repeat business and new customers from recommendations.
- **USP potential** – superior quality will help attract customers over rivals.
- **Pricing flexibility** – may enable higher prices, thus higher margins.
- **Cost minimisation** – less waste, re-working, re-testing, re-inspecting poor quality products, less time handling complaints, lost sales, legal action and compensation from dissatisfied customers.
- **Recruitment and retention** – easier to attract and retain good quality staff.
- **Achievement of objectives** re: sales, market share, customer loyalty, profit.

The Distinction between Quality Control and Quality Assurance

Quality control: the process of inspecting and testing products in order to reduce the number of rejects in the production process and returns from customers; involves measuring performance against known standards, which should be based on customer expectations.

Quality assurance: more than the inspection and testing procedures associated with quality control; involves a comprehensive, structured approach to quality, including planning for prevention of poor quality.

Quality Control:

Involves assessing **product characteristics** or **behaviour of person** (if service) against performance standards eg through physical observation. Individual workers should, ideally, be responsible for checking quality at every stage of production, **not** a separate quality control inspector - avoids time lag between fault being detected + chance of faulty products reaching customers. *Thus*, minimises wastage, reworking, customer dissatisfaction. Increased responsibility can also enhance motivation (Herzberg).

Quality Assurance: *Involves establishing:*

- **effective processes** for converting customer needs into products and processes for their achievement.
- **efficient systems** for determining capability and effectiveness of processes, detecting and correcting errors / deviations.
- **appropriate measures of performance** for control of processes.

Ideally, should involve identifying, discussing, selecting, and implementing ways to improve quality on an **ongoing** basis.

Systems of Quality Assurance

Systems of quality assurance: approaches used to achieve quality.

Total Quality Management (TQM): a proactive, systematic, strategic approach to management; involves all employees and all aspects of the business in meeting or exceeding customer expectations, both externally and internally, with staff regarded as internal customers.

Kaizen: a Japanese word that means continuous improvement, which is a key feature of TQM; usually involves groups of workers that meet regularly to discuss how work-related tasks can be completed more efficiently.

Kaizen groups and quality circles: groups of workers, (usually between 3 and 12), who meet regularly to identify and discuss problems, consider alternative solutions, and make recommendations to management. Members are usually drawn from the same work area but may include an engineer, quality inspector and member of the sales team - to enable problems to be viewed from all angles.

What is TQM? *A theoretically perfectly managed organisation, with:*

- mission, vision and values understood by all, that underpin decision-making.
- 'customer focused' staff - key role to meet customers' (int & ext) expectations.
- continuous improvement (kaizen) - to increase customer satisfaction.
- 'fact based' decision-making - not taken on hunch or biased.
- unencumbered lateral and vertical communications.
- no reluctance or fear amongst staff in putting forward suggestions.
- quality standards in place, variations identified and corrective action taken.
- problems not seen negatively, but as an opportunity for improvement.
- appropriately trained, empowered, compensated staff.
- management who coach, train and support the workforce, rather than the traditional dictatorial / supervisory approach.

All management & staff know their 'customers', care and take pride in their work, are involved in **continuous improvement** of products / processes, aim *'to do the right thing, first time'*. Top management take strategic decisions, but tactical and operational decisions delegated to empowered, capable, motivated employees.

Potential Benefits: *TQM helps to...*

- **minimise cost** of poor quality - materials, labour, lost sales.
- **improve motivation** and **efficiency** in the long-run.
- **attract/retain good staff** - easier, cheaper recruitment, lower labour turnover.

Issues Involved:

- **Staff reluctance** - to inform other staff / colleagues that their work is sub-standard.
- **Management reluctance** - to delegate responsibility and empower staff.
- **Training** - to ensure capable, responsible staff, change attitudes, overcome barriers.
- **Changing attitudes** - difficult, time consuming.
- **Ongoing investment in market research** - to identify (changing) customer requirements.
- **Costs** - of training, market research; staff may also demand **more pay** for extra responsibility.
- **Adapting recruitment and selection policies** - to secure responsible, self-motivated individuals, that fit in 'empowered' culture.
- **Disruption to production** eg kaizen groups or quality circles remove workers from production for periods at a time - requires careful planning, scheduling to minimise disruption.

Quality Standards

Quality standards: established criteria against which performance in terms of meeting customer requirements is assessed.
BS 5750: the British standard on quality management systems. **EN 29000:** the European standard. **ISO 9001:** the International standard.

Achieving Quality Standards Certification:

To achieve BS 5750, EN 29000 or ISO 9001 certification the organisation must document, implement and maintain a quality management system, and continually improve its effectiveness in accordance with the requirements laid down by the relevant quality standard. This involves:

- establishing processes / best practices to ensure quality (ie that customer requirements met).
- determining criteria and methods to ensure effective operation and control of these processes.
- documenting evidence of the above.
- providing the necessary resources and info to enable the effective operation, monitoring and control of processes.
- monitoring, measuring, analysing & reviewing processes to assess effectiveness through regular checks (audits).
- taking appropriate, corrective action to rectify any problems and achieve targets / results planned.
- striving to continually improve these processes.

A business must **prove it does what it says it does** to an independent, objective third party – a 'registrar' from a recognised awarding body. The registrar reviews documentation and interviews management and staff to check the quality management system documented is being effectively implemented, and awards certification.

Possible Benefits:

Marketing: Certification can instil confidence amongst target market, help gain sales, maximise revenues, market share; should also ensure customer requirements met, customer satisfaction maximised, help secure repeat business, maximise sales, market share.

HR: May help attract and retain good quality staff - easier and cheaper recruitment, minimise labour turnover and associated costs.

Operational and Financial: Likely to increase productivity and efficiency in the long-run, minimise costs by eliminating waste, costly errors, chance of litigation, etc. With higher revenues (from marketing advantages above), should ultimately lead to higher profits.

Issues Involved:

- **Time consuming** – certification can take up to one year.
- **Documentary evidence / paperwork** – can get in way of making genuine quality improvements.
- **Can be costly** – to design, implement, monitor and control the system designed, especially if use quality consultant.
- **May require significant changes** – to existing policies, procedures, practices - can lead to resistance amongst staff and management.
- **Overcoming resistance** – can be time consuming, delay whole process, and necessitate investment in training to change attitudes and provide the info and skills required to adhere to the system designed, and identify, eliminate and prevent quality problems.

DEVELOPING EFFECTIVE OPERATIONS: CUSTOMER SERVICE
Methods of Meeting Customer Expectations

Customer expectations: the beliefs that purchasers of products or services hold about the product / service they are buying; may concern product / service attributes, but also other aspects relating to the sale eg price, credit terms, delivery times, after sales service, etc.

Customer requirements: what the potential buyer of a product or service needs or wants when they buy a particular product / service.

Overview:

Meeting customer expectations is fundamental to the success of every business. If customers' expectations are not met this will lead to dissatisfied customers, lack of repeat business, and failure to gain new customers from recommendations.

It is only by meeting customer **requirements** that customer **expectations** will be met. *This involves:*

- finding out what customers need / want.
- designing a product / service to meet these needs / wants.
- securing the resources required to produce the product / service to meet these needs / wants.
- implementing systems and procedures to ensure customer needs / wants are consistently met.

Role of Training, Education, Communication:

Standards of performance (based on customer requirements), need to be communicated to those expected to achieve them.

Importance of meeting customer requirements to long-term success (and job security), should be communicated to staff - to encourage commitment to meeting customer expectations.

Training may be essential to ensure staff possess the knowledge, skills and attitudes required to produce the product / service designed to meet customer requirements / expectations.

Role of Market Research: *Essential in:*

- finding out what customers require.
- designing product / service to meet these requirements.
- testing if product / service meets requirements prior to full launch.
- obtaining customer feedback post purchase to assess extent to which requirements met, enable weaknesses to be addressed.
- identifying changing customer requirements, enabling timely and appropriate action to ensure customer expectations continually met.

Role of Quality Control and Assurance Systems:

Quality control involves measuring performance against established standards for performance, based on customer expectations. Detection of errors prior to a product / service reaching the customer is vital to ensure expectations are met. Ideally, errors should be prevented from occurring in the first place, through quality assurance systems such as TQM - to eliminate the need for re-work and failure to meet expectations re: delivery times.

The Need to Provide Accurate, Up-to-date Descriptions:

Expectations may be based on what past customers have said <u>and</u> on what the business says. *Thus,* descriptions need to be accurate and precise, and promises made must be kept (re quality, delivery, etc).

© APT Initiatives Ltd, 2011

Monitoring and Improving Customer Service

Customer service: a series of activities designed to maximise the level of satisfaction customers gain from purchasing a product or service from a business. It may concern the service given to customers before, during, and after purchase.

Methods for Monitoring Customer service:

Direct:
- Setting up systems for customer feedback eg surveys, forums, suggestion boxes.
- Reviewing any complaints / compliment letters received.
- Recording and listening to telephone conversations between customers and staff.
- Using mystery shoppers / guests / diners.

Indirect:
- Reviewing level of sales volumes, repeat business, new customers.
- Reviewing level of staff turnover.
- *But…* changes in above may not be related to customer service - need follow-up investigation to determine underlying cause.

The Benefits of High Levels of Customer Service

Satisfied customers, resulting in…

- …**repeat customers**, high **customer retention, loyalty** - maintaining sales, market share.
- …**new customers** through recommendations - building customer base, sales, market share.
- …**fewer complaints**, *thus* less time, effort, money wasted handling complaints.
- …**positive working atmosphere,** *thus* reduced labour turnover and associated costs.

Also:
- **professional public image** - help gain customers, attract employees + potential investors.
- **competitive edge** - USP - service may be valued more by some customers than price.

Overall, helps **maximise sales, market share, minimises costs** <u>and</u> **increases profits** – as long as cost of providing high levels of customer service do not outweigh benefits.

Improving Customer Service:

- **Customer and employee forums** - to suggest ways on how to improve.
- **Customer focus groups** (10 to 20) meet / surveyed regularly - asked to put forward ideas on how to improve, rewarded through pay, gift vouchers, free products, etc.
- **Dedicated customer service policies and practices** including dedicated customer helpline.
- **Website with FAQ's** - providing access / support 24 hours a day.
- **Timely admission and apology** for any mistakes.
- **Sensitive, careful, quick, complete handling of complaints**.
- **Training all staff in contact with customers** - to be polite, courteous, flexible, and ensure specific improvements are made.
- **Disciplinary action** - if staff do not meet requirements (despite training).
- **Staff bonuses or incentives** - to encourage improvements.

WORKING WITH SUPPLIERS

Choosing Effective Suppliers

Suppliers: Individuals, businesses, or other organisations that provide resource inputs (eg materials, components, equipment, energy, etc) to other individuals, businesses, or organisations that need them, in order to supply their customers with the goods or services they require.

Types of Goods / Services Supplied:

- equipment and machinery.
- vehicles.
- raw materials.
- component parts inserted into more complex products.
- gas and electricity (energy).
- petrol (fuel).
- stationery.
- temporary labour (hired through agencies).

Capital equipment, vehicles bought infrequently or leased permanently. Other items bought repeatedly - strong case for building relationship with trusted suppliers.

Factors to Consider when Choosing Suppliers:

- Price
- Payment / credit terms
- Quality
- Capacity & lead time (delivery)
- Reliability
- Financial stability
- Flexibility
- Location
- Ethical & environmental considerations

Most important factor will vary according to needs, priorities, situation, *eg:*

- With raw materials - **quality** is key – has direct impact on sales, profit.
- For firms on very low margins – low **price** important.
- If uncertain about demand + little storage capacity – **lead time** and **flexibility** is important.

With **'just in time'** production – **flexibility** and **reliability** are important.

Role in Improving Operational Performance

Operational performance: concerns unit costs, quality, output / productivity, wastage, effectiveness in meeting delivery / lead times, capacity utilisation.

Role in Achieving Quality:

The quality of a firm's product / service is dependent upon the quality of inputs used to produce them, particularly supplies of raw materials / components used to produce a tangible, physical product.

Meeting Delivery Times, Maximising Productivity & Capacity Utilisation:

The more reliable the supplier (quality, quantity), the more able the business is to meet delivery times, and the less stoppages in production as a result of poor quality supplies, or stockout.

Role in Cutting Costs, Wastage:

- The lower suppliers' **prices** the lower the **unit costs**.
- **Consistent quality** supplies reduces **waste** and associated costs.
- **Reliable** suppliers maximise productivity, capacity utilisation - minimising **fixed costs** per unit.
- **Flexible, reliable** suppliers able to deliver 'just-in-time' reduce **stockholding costs**.
- Lower unit costs enables **lower prices**.

Key role in developing / maintaining **competitive edge** through lower prices, superior quality, or faster delivery.

USING TECHNOLOGY IN OPERATIONS

Types and Benefits of Technology in Operations Management

Technology: the combination of skills, knowledge, tools, equipment, machines and computers used to undertake tasks.

Robotics: the use of mechanical devices with three or more axes that move automatically to carry out operational tasks unsupervised.

Automation: the use of mechanical devices to carry out operational tasks.

Communications technology: the combination of skills, knowledge, tools, equipment, machines and computers used in the process of transferring information between people.

Design technology: the combination of skills, knowledge, tools, equipment, machines and computers used in the process of designing products and services.

General Benefits of Using Technology in Operations:

- Perform tasks previously undertaken by highly skilled labour, *thus,* **reducing labour costs.**
- More precise, reliable, consistent, make fewer mistakes than humans, *thus* **improved quality, less waste** & associated costs.
- Quicker than humans, which with greater precision and less rework, can **increase productivity, efficiency.**

Reduced costs, improved quality, productivity - provides **marketing advantages** / a **competitive edge,** maximises **sales, profits.** *Eg:*

- **Reduced costs** enables lower selling price to increase sales (depending on PED), or higher margins.
- **Improvements in quality** helps gain repeat business and new customers (from recommendations), *thus* greater sales, profits.
- **Improvements in productivity** enables new products or orders to be actioned more quickly - helps win customers over rivals, plus enables more orders to be taken on - maximising capacity utilisation and reducing unit costs.

Robotics:

Reduce the need for humans to perform dangerous, dirty, boring and repetitive tasks. Main advantages over humans: **speed, strength, ability to withstand extreme conditions.**

Used extensively in car manufacturing. *Industrial uses:*
- materials transport - heavy or hazardous materials.
- welding - fastening metal together (heat and pressure).
- assembly - fitting together parts into unified whole.
- painting, including spray finishing.
- inspecting and testing products.

Environmental applications: cleaning contaminated sites.

Non-industrial applications:
- security - airport surveillance.
- commercial cleaning.
- food services.
- health care - assist physically handicapped, the elderly.
- space exploration.

Automation:

- Prevalent in manufacturing, eg **computer-aided manufacture (CAM):** computers control and adjust production; manufacture products in shorter times, with improved quality and reliability, *thus* lower costs.
- Major role in increasing productivity and reducing costs in services eg **self-scanning checkouts** in supermarkets.
- Automation of **information** (as opposed to labour) increasingly common eg **automated stock control systems** (see below), **'Manufacturing Resource Planning' software** - quickly find out whether order can be fulfilled with existing capacity, in time available.

Automated stock control: Laser scanning devices scan bar codes of stock arriving in business, pass this information to a central computer that stores details of stock levels. Any items leaving the business as sales or disposals are also scanned, and details are fed back to central computer, which automatically updates stock figures held. With **Electronic Data Interchange (EDI)** info on sales and stock can be passed to suppliers enabling orders to be generated automatically, and deliveries to arrive as and when required ('just-in-time'). *Benefits:*

- Reduces times stock has to be manually counted, *thus* **faster ordering, reduced labour costs.**
- **Minimises stock loss** – greater accuracy of ordering leads to fewer reductions and disposals (from over ordering).
- **Minimises storage costs** – up to date stock figures enables faster ordering and means less buffer stock required 'just-in-case'.
- More accurate ordering also **minimises customer dissatisfaction** from poor availability, and **potential loss in sales, profits.**

Communications Technology:
Application of IT to communications has speeded up transmission of information, enabled **faster decision-making, reduced costs**. *Eg:*

- **Email (electronic mail)** – documents sent to several people at same time, received almost instantly - enables faster decisions, saves on printing, stationery, postage, travel costs.
- **Voice Over Internet Protocol (VoiP)** – costs less to make calls than landlines, mobile.
- **Mobile phones** – reach recipients not at usual place; text, pictures - no need to be near PC.
- **Smartphones** – mobile phones with PC capability, eg IPhone, Blackberry.
- **Audio/tele/video/web conferencing** and **VoiP technologies** – meetings/presentations can take place between people in different locations - eliminates travel time/costs, rental costs, organising/planning time - increased productivity, faster communication & decision making.

Above technologies have enabled **homeworking / teleworking** (work whilst travelling):
- **Lowers fixed costs** - less work space required resulting in **lower rents.**
- **Frees up work space** for **more productive (profitable) use**.

Also made cross-border communication easier - enabled businesses to **reduce fixed** and **variable costs** by **relocating** to **cheaper areas**.

Design Technology:

Computer-aided design (CAD): Used to design 2D & 3D virtual models - product simulated on computer screen, design altered without building prototype. Used to design cars, ships, aeroplanes, houses, other buildings, and produce animation for movies, adverts, technical manuals. *Benefits:*

- **Reduces cost** and **time in new product development** - more affordable, feasible.

- Enables **more rapid response to changes** in market - helps business gain / maintain market share.

Issues in Introducing and Updating Technology

Effect on Staff:

- **Job security / livelihood** – can lead to redundancies, feelings of insecurity amongst staff who remain.
- **Skills obsolescence, loss of status, inability to do chosen field of work / preferred tasks** – may lead to job dissatisfaction. (NB meaningful, interesting work, Herzberg's motivator).
- **The need to learn new skills** – some staff may find this difficult, lack competence, confidence, feelings of inadequacy, insecurity.
- **Changes to work groups / social relationships** – negatively affecting satisfaction of social needs (Maslow).

Negative effect on staff can be significant and affect **morale, motivation and performance**. Change of any kind associated with uncertainty, feelings of anxiety – can only be reduced if reasons fully communicated.

Management Attitudes:

Employees' roles may change from operational to supervisory. Managers may struggle to empower staff, due to concerns about capability, or concerns over relinquishing power.

May overcome former by appointing workers with capabilities from **outside** the business. Latter requires fundamental change in attitudes, which can be difficult.

Training...

...to ensure staff have the knowledge and skills required to operate or supervise the new technologies.

...to change management attitudes to empower employees to take on more responsible / supervisory roles.

Health Issues: New technologies have brought new health concerns and new legislation eg regular breaks, specialist equipment to minimise risk of RSI, poor vision from computer glare, back problems from poorly designed chairs. This has **increased costs.**

Costs and Availability of Finance:

Implementing new technologies may incur: **capital, installation, training costs, redundancy pay.** Also, **running costs.** *But*…These costs should be outweighed in the long-run by the reduction in costs, increased productivity, and marketing advantages outlined above.

Due to rapid pace of technological change, life of new technologies is shorter and shorter, businesses may have to plan annually to invest in new technologies, but it can be difficult to predict and budget for the cost.

Specific Issues with Communications Technologies:

- **Potential IT skill shortages** – Developments in ICT, internet and e-commerce - need people with well-developed IT skills.
- **Mechanical faults / breakdowns** – complete loss of information.
- **Information / communication overload** – receiver unable to process all the information sent.
- **Security / confidentiality** eg information sent via e-mail or fax often easily accessed / viewed by others.
- **Non-business use** of office emails – reducing productivity.

MARKETING & THE COMPETITIVE ENVIRONMENT

EFFECTIVE MARKETING

The Purpose of Marketing

Marketing: the management process responsible for getting the right product / service to customers at the right price, in the right place, at the right time; involves identifying, anticipating and satisfying customer requirements.

Role & Purpose:

To identify, anticipate and, ultimately, **satisfy customer requirements**:

- **Identifying** - market research to identify customer needs / wants.
- **Anticipating** - making assumptions, predictions based on market research.
- **Satisfying** - designing and providing customers with a product / service that meets their requirements, making them aware of it, enabling them to access it, selling it at a price they are able and willing to pay.

To **fulfil organisational objectives** eg maximise sales revenue, market share, and most importantly (for most businesses), profit.

Marketing is the most co-ordinating and integrating process within a firm. It looks at the business and its activities through the eyes of customers. Information collected on customers and the external business environment (through market research) is communicated throughout other functional areas. Hence, role of marketing also involves:

- communicating regularly with Finance personnel - to ensure sufficient funds are available to fulfil marketing objectives.
- liaising closely with HR personnel - to ensure sufficient no. of people with the right knowledge, skills, are obtained to meet customer requirements.
- liaising closely with Production / Operations - to ensure products produced (in line with customer specifications), in right quantities, at right time.

Summary of The Marketing process

Researching the Market
Gathering info on customers, competitors, environment

Determining Marketing Objectives & Strategy
Identifying customer requirements, deciding how to meet these and overall business objectives

Producing the Product
Deciding product features - size, quality, packaging

Pricing the Product
at a price customers willing / able to pay + makes a profit

Placing the Product
Location, distribution channels

Promoting the Product
PR, advertising, personal selling, sales promotion

Monitoring and Evaluating Results
via market research, sales & financial data

& Modifying Objectives and Strategies
ie decisions re: product, price, promotion, place, in light of results and changing external environment

Niche and Mass Marketing

Market segment: a group of customers within an entire market that share similar needs and wants and common characteristics.

Niche marketing: identifying and satisfying a relatively small segment of the market, eg customers in a particular geographical area, of a particular age group, with a particular hobby or interest, with a particular need eg food free from nuts.

Mass marketing: aiming products or services at whole markets, or most of a market, rather than particular market segments. Generally concerns products that everyone (or almost everyone) buys at some point, eg food, clothes, mobile phones, cars.

Niche Marketing:

Potential Benefits	Drawbacks / Limitations
• Fewer competitors.	• Less potential revenue.
• Greater scope to charge higher price.	• Limited economies - higher unit costs.
• Requires fewer resources, *thus* less investment.	• Lower potential profit (due to above).
	• Longer to recoup R&D costs.
	• More vulnerable to small fall in demand / loss of a few customers.

Mass Marketing:

Potential Benefits	Drawbacks / Limitations
• Greater potential revenue.	• Needs more capacity, resources, capital, risk.
• Greater economies - lower unit costs	• More competition.
• Higher profit (due to above).	• Less scope to charge higher prices.
• Faster to recoup R&D costs.	• High promotion costs.
• Less vulnerable to small fall in demand / loss of a few customers.	

Consumer Marketing & Business to Business Marketing

Consumer marketing: marketing to the general public ie private individuals or families (as opposed to other businesses).

Business to business marketing: marketing to other businesses (as opposed to the general public ie private individuals or families).

Area	B2B Marketing	B2C Marketing
Customers	**Small** number of **large** customers.	**Large** number of **small** customers.
Market research	Based on **interviews** - perhaps using **census** rather than sample.	**Sample** surveys.
Order size	**Large**.	**Small**.
Product	Often **customised**.	Usually **standardised**.
Price	Usually **negotiated**.	Usually **fixed** (by seller).
Promotion	**Personal selling** plays **large** role. Use of **informative** as opposed to persuasive **adverts** - as buyers are more knowledgeable, rational - base decisions **on factual info**.	**Personal selling** plays **minor** role. Use of **persuasive adverts** and **sales promotion** - as buyers are less rational, knowledgeable.
Place / Distribution	Sales normally **direct** without intermediaries.	Sales often through **indirect** channels ie through intermediaries.

Levels / standards of **customer service** may also be higher in B2B marketing - generally higher expectations than consumers.

DESIGNING AN EFFECTIVE MARKETING MIX

Influences on the Marketing Mix

Marketing mix: consists of four basic elements, namely, product, price, place and promotion; concerns the tactics a business uses in order to meet customer requirements and, ultimately, achieve marketing and overall business objectives.

Marketing Mix Components:

Basic Mix – 4 P's:

Product, Price, Place, Promotion.

7 P's (especially relevant to **services***):*

- **Physical evidence** - design, layout and décor of buildings, facilities provided eg toilets, car parking.

- **Process** - systems used for ordering / booking, paying, including customer contact before, during, or after service / despatch / receipt.

- **People** - ability, attitudes, behaviour of staff in contact with customers.

Influences on the Marketing Mix:

- **Marketing & overall (corporate) objectives:** Eg increasing market share may require changes to product quality, lower price, more promotion, better access - to make more customers able and willing to buy.

- **Customer requirements** – the most influential factor: Mix must be designed with customer requirements in mind, else risks failure to satisfy customers and fulfil business objectives

- **Competitor activities, strengths and weaknesses:** Mix needs to be designed to stand out from rivals and adapted in light of changing competitor activities.

- **Costs involved and amount of finance available:** Influences ability to introduce new products, modify existing ones, type / level of promotion and distribution used, and (especially) decisions over price.

- **Findings from market research** re customer needs / preferences, competitors, costs: Essential to design a product that most closely matches customer requirements, determine price customers willing and able to pay, most appropriate location / distribution channel(s), most effective methods of promotion.

- **Technology:** Influences development of new products / services, how often updates required, promotion and distribution used (eg internet, websites, email), as well as enabling businesses to invest in new cost saving machinery and equipment - provides greater flexibility over price.

- **Size and capability of workforce and existing plant and machinery:** May constrain NPD or promotional methods (in short-term). The more multi-skilled the workforce and flexible the plant / machinery, the more able to develop new products / respond to changing customer needs. The more productive the workforce and existing plant and machinery, the lower the costs and the greater the flexibility over price.

- **Changes in other external factors:** Eg changes in **legislation** affect decisions re product and promotion – to ensure compliance with product safety and advertising standards. **social attitudes** - such as - increasing concern re the environment affect decisions over packaging; **economic factors** - such as - changes in interest or taxation rates affect disposable income, level of demand, and influence decisions over price.

The Importance of an Integrated Marketing Mix

Integrated marketing mix: where all the separate elements (of product, price, promotion and place) blend together to form a unified whole; requires each separate element of the mix to support and be consistent with the other elements of the mix.

Importance of an Integrated Mix:

Some firms place emphasis on one particular aspect. *However,* all aspects will still be addressed, as all remain important to the customer. Customers need a product / service that:

- meets their needs (product / service).
- they can afford / provides value for money (price).
- they are fully aware of and informed about (promotion).
- they can access conveniently (place / distribution).

A business will make decisions about each aspect of the mix, but the mix needs to be blended effectively to achieve the desired result in terms of sales, market share, profit, etc. If a business fails to address one particular aspect, or to ensure that each separate element supports and is consistent with other elements of the mix, they are unlikely to be successful in the long-term.

Achieving an Integrated Marketing Mix:

Requires each element to support and be consistent with the other elements. Important to recognise interrelationship - changes in one element affects another, *eg:*

- **Product & price:** Price must cover total costs in long-term. Greater flexibility in short-term.
- **Product life-cycle & price:** High price may be appropriate at start - consumers prepared to pay premium for unique product. Maturity or decline reduce price to maintain market share.
- **Product & promotion:** If use / benefits obvious, simple to understand, personal selling unnecessary waste of resources – more appropriate for complex, technical products.
- **Product life-cycle & promotion:** Advertising, sales promotion is widely used during launch and growth - essential to generate awareness, persuade customers to buy.
- **Product & place / distribution:** Bulky, fragile, perishable, tailored, complex product need a direct channel.
- **Promotion & price:** Cost of promotion and way product is promoted affects selling price, eg advertising can add perceived value - allows higher prices to be charged.
- **Promotion & place / distribution:** Intermediaries need return. Price too low won't stock it.

Getting the right blend / balance essentially requires:

- **Market research:** Test marketing to determine if marketing mix will achieve desired results.
- **Creativity** - to stand out from rivals; **organisational culture** that encourages **innovation**.
- **Adaptability:** Customer needs, preferences, perceptions change, ongoing customer research / feedback vital, with **flexible organisational structure** to enable timely response.
- Consideration of **financial and human resources** available to the business - to ensure mix not designed that stretches resources to the limit, and risks the business's very survival.

USING THE MARKETING MIX: PRODUCT

Influences on the Development of New goods and Services

New product development: where a business creates a new good or service, or modifies an existing good or service in line with changes in the market place.

Goods: tangible ie physical objects that can be seen and touched, eg food, shampoo, car, computer, textbook, pen.

Services: things other people do for you, eg cutting your hair, looking after your money, prescribing treatment when you are ill. They are intangible ie cannot be seen or touched.

Reasons / Benefits of NPD:

Completely new products may be essential in helping to:

- spread risk.
- achieve objectives re: market leadership, market share.
- replace declining, unpopular, obsolete products.
- overcome problems of seasonality.
- build upon the success of a previous product / brand.

Existing products may also be adapted to:

- meet customer needs more closely - maximise sales, market share, raise price - maximise profits / profitability.
- make product stand out from rivals - gain sales, share.
- cut costs eg through cheaper materials (without affecting customer satisfaction) - increase profits / profitability.
- make better use of resources / increase capacity utilisation - reduce fixed costs per unit, increase profits / margins.

Types of New Goods and Services:

- **'New to the world'** - often scientific, technological developments - enable purchasers to do something previously not possible, or more efficient or superior way of doing things eg mobile phones, digital cameras.
- **New to the business but not to the world** - business produces own version of product of another business often a rival.
- **Modification of existing good / service** eg new feature, size, function.

Basic Requirements: All new products should fulfil 3 basic criteria:

1. be **functionally sound** - fit for purpose bought to satisfy.
2. be **aesthetically sound** - visually appealing.
3. be **capable of economic production** - able to make sufficient profit at a price customers are able and willing to pay.

Relative importance will vary according to product and markets served, eg:

- machines in factory - more capable of doing job than visually appealing.
- clothes in developed economies - emphasis on aesthetics over function.
- cars - often purchased according to both criteria equally.

Key Stages Involves in Developing New Goods / Services

Identification of new product ideas / Idea generation
Screening and selection of new product ideas
Concept development and testing
Business analysis – determining price, demand, break-even, profitability
More detailed testing of the product and consumer reaction
Technical implementation – preparation for full launch
Full launch

Factors Influencing the Development of New Goods / Services:

- **Customer requirements** – the purpose of marketing is to design a product / service that satisfies these.
- **Competitor activities** – ideas for new products often stem from observing / investigating competitors.
- **Technology** – creates new products / markets, and influence how often product needs updating.
- **Legislation** – new products must comply with product safety legislation.
- **Social attitudes / trends** – concern over environment may influence materials, processes used; changes in tastes, fashion influences the design of clothes, hair, cars, mobile phones.
- **Marketing and overall business objectives** eg NPD might be integral to market leadership, increasing sales or market share may trigger improvements to existing products, profit maximisation might result in products being modified to make them cheaper to produce.
- **Entrepreneurial skills of owners / managers** – ability to spot gaps, vision to appreciate potential of new technological developments.
- **Resources and costs involved and availability of finance and other resources** – costs and finance available influence firm's ability to introduce new products, modify existing ones. The more **multi-skilled** the workforce and **flexible** existing plant and machinery, the more able the firm is to develop **new products** to meet new / changing customer needs.
- **Findings from market research** – highly influential role in NPD - may initially identify gaps in market, then obtain customer feedback, resulting in product modifications, help assess demand at price proposed and, ultimately, determine profitability. Provides crucial information that has a major influence on whether or not a new product idea is developed and launched.
- **Opportunity cost** – new product only worthwhile if it is more profitable than the alternatives that will be sacrificed.

Unique Selling Points (or Propositions)

Unique selling points: characteristics of products / services that differentiate them from similar products / services in the market place.

Benefits of USP's:

USP's are what makes a business's product or service **stand out** from that of rivals so that customers are attracted to buy it. *Thus,* USP's are important in **achieving objectives** relating to **sales, market share, customer loyalty** and, ultimately, **profit.** USP's may also enable **higher prices** to be charged - resulting in **higher profits / profitability.**

Examples of USP's:

- **Better performance / functional superiority** eg quicker, more economical, longer-lasting, more environmentally friendly, tastier and healthier (food).
- **Extra features** eg built in SATNAV in cars, Jacuzzi bath in hotel bedroom.
- **Better appearance / more aesthetically pleasing** or **fashionable** – cars, clothes.
- **Better packaging** – greater protection, help product stand out on shelves.
- **Higher standards of service** eg faster delivery, more attentive, capable staff, more convenient opening hours or location, better credit terms, longer guarantees.
- **Lowest price.**
- **Perceived (psychological) advantages** – through branding and advertising.

Product Portfolio Analysis

Product portfolio: the total range of products or brands produced by a single business.

Product line: a group of products sold by a business with similar characteristics, similar uses or sold to the same type of customer eg different models of cars, brands of detergent sold by the same business.

Product portfolio analysis: the examination of all a business's products or brands to identify their strengths, potential, and weaknesses.

Boston matrix: a tool of product portfolio analysis - classifies a business's products according to market share and rate of market growth.

The Boston Matrix

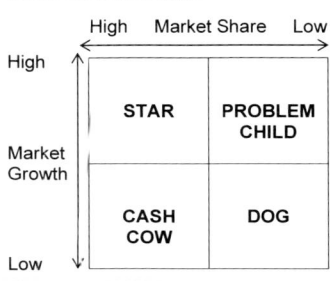

Problem Child	Star	Cash Cow	Dog
Low market share in rapid growth market. Need protection to keep position + high investment to achieve growth. New products usually begin here. Uncertainty about their future - risk.	Large share of high growth market. Generate high revenue but require high investment in promotion and possibly capacity - to maintain dominant position. Cash flow can be low, even negative.	High market share in low growth market. Often well established products - require less investment in promotion, and R&D, and other start-up costs likely to have been recovered. Excellent cash generators - often used to fund new products.	Small share of low growth / stagnant market. Should not necessarily be dropped - revenue and profit may still be significant, may also be essential part of product range, and / or scope for revival.

Use	Limitations
Can help a business to arrange product portfolio to **balance growth, cash flow and risk** – need to balance dogs and stars (high investment, drain resources) with cash cows, where R&D costs recovered, cost of promotion low in comparison to sales, and healthy profit and cash flow realised.	• Can prove **difficult, time consuming** and **expensive** to obtain accurate data on market size, growth, share - especially for small business with limited time and money to invest in market research. • Concerned with present and immediate future - **less useful in the longer term.** Predictions about future market growth and market share may be more important than that already recorded / achieved. • Does not take into account other factors vitally important in product decisions eg **contribution to total sales and profit, significance as part of wider product range.**

Product Life Cycles

Product life cycle: refers to the different stages through which a product passes and the levels of sales experienced at each stage.
Extension strategy: a method used to extend the life of a product.

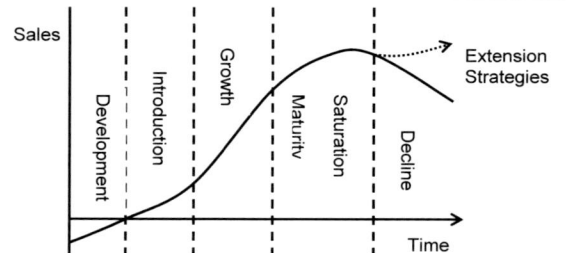

Use: PLC analysis can help firm make decisions re: promotion, price, when to use extension strategies, when to remove product from market.

Extension Strategies:

- Change design, image, appearance, packaging, ingredients.
- Increase frequency of use eg promote health benefits.
- Attract new users / target new markets.
- Develop alternative/new uses.
- Add additional models / wider range.
- Extend product into other formats.

Limitations: Knowledge of what is currently happening does not guarantee success – still need to select right strategies and implement these successfully. Also, no two life cycles the same - difficult to forecast accurately; difficult to determine where product lies. Variations in sales occur year to year - vital not to misinterpret fluctuations to mean product is in decline. Success depends upon firm making good use of information on: **sales, customer attitudes and opinions, competitor activities, life cycle of similar products,** and **economic factors** that may affect sales in the future.

Development	Introduction	Growth	Maturity & Saturation	Decline
Ideas investigated, designed, tested, selected. Marketing plan prepared. High R&D and resource costs. No cash inflows from sales, only cash outflows. The more novel the product the longer this stage.	Product launched. Price high or low, depending on uniqueness and firm's objectives. Often high investment in promotion. Sales volume and capacity utilisation (CU) often low, thus high fixed costs per unit. Unlikely to be profitable, and cash flow negative.	Growing awareness, rising sales & CU, *thus* lower fixed costs per unit. Promotion cost also spread over greater output, *thus* positive cash flow, rapidly rising profits, *but* attracts competition. Often requires changes to strategy to supply wider market and make it hard for competitors to secure foothold.	**Maturity:** Sales & CU continue to rise, *thus* cash flow and profits continue to rise. *But,* rate of growth slows, begins to level off - as competition intensifies. Promotion defensive and increased investment - to maintain market share. Extension strategies planned. **Saturation:** Market stops growing., sales level off, most people have bought, or are buying at a rate unlikely to increase. Often too many firms competing for too few customers.	Sales fall, low CU, falling cash flows and profits. May be lucrative if marketing effort withdrawn. If product damaging image / reputation, or cash flows negative and no contribution to FC and profit, then product withdrawn.

USING THE MARKETING MIX: PROMOTION

Elements of the Promotional Mix

Promotion: communication techniques aimed at informing, influencing and persuading customers to buy or use a firm's products / services.

Promotional mix: the combination of communication techniques a business uses to inform, influence and persuade customers to buy or use its products or services.

Above the line methods of promotion: techniques that involve communicating with customers through independent media, ie media over which the business has little direct control and where there is no direct contact with the customer, eg TV, radio, newspaper advertising.

Below the line methods of promotion: techniques that do not involve communicating with customers through independent media, but through the use of methods over which the firm has some degree of control, eg direct mail, personal selling.

PR (Public Relations): concerns effectively managing relationships with different publics of significance to the business, mainly through news media such as press, television, radio.

Sponsorship: a form of public relations activity which involves funding for people or events, for example, relating to sports or the arts, in order to get the business name or brand names associated with particular activities, and secure wide media coverage and public awareness.

Branding: involves giving a distinctive name, term, symbol, image, design or packaging to a product (or group of products), which enables it to be easily recognised and differentiates it from other products.

Packaging: the outer wrapper or container of a product which is often an indication of the quality of the product itself; plays an important part in the promotion of a product and may help to persuade a customer to buy it.

Merchandising: often refers to the selection of products on display and, in particular, the way in which these products are displayed in places where customers make purchases ie buy a good or use a service.

Sales promotions: short-term incentives eg price discounts, free samples, to persuade customers to buy a particular product and / or distributors (eg retailers and wholesalers) to stock a particular product.

Personal selling: involves sales staff making oral presentations to, and / or taking part in discussions with, potential customers of a product or service, either face to face or by telephone, with the purpose of making a sale.

Direct marketing: sending promotional messages direct to carefully targeted customers, ie without the use of other channels of communication such as TV, newspapers and radio. It includes **direct mail**, **email marketing**, **text message marketing**, and **telesales**.

Advertising: the process of communicating promotional messages to customers through paid media eg newspapers, television, radio.

Internet advertising: sending promotional messages to customers through the global computer network (the Internet).

Direct response marketing: communicating with customers about a product / service, with the aim of obtaining an immediate response.

© **APT Initiatives Ltd**, 2011

Objectives of promotion:

1. To raise or maintain customer awareness.
2. To generate interest.
3. To stimulate desire.
4. To encourage action / To make sales.
5. To provide reassurance and secure repeat business.
6. To encourage customer loyalty.
7. To improve the image of a business.

Linked with the above:

8. To differentiate a business, its products/services from rivals.

Public Relations:

Activities:

- Securing press / news releases.
- Giving donations to charities.
- Providing sponsorship - funding for people or events eg relating to sports, the arts.
- Obtaining product endorsements - where a public figure / celebrity show support for / approval of a firm's product(s).

Overall aim:

- To increase / maximise sales by improving the image of a business and its products / services.

Specific objectives:

- To obtain media coverage of a key event eg product launch.
- To generate word of mouth interest.

Benefits: Relatively cheap way to reach many customers; Message viewed more 'credible' if sent by 3rd party.

Drawbacks: Cannot always control what is printed or said.

Branding: More than a distinctive name.
Often supported by logos, slogans, or catchlines.

Benefits: *Helps to…*

- make a product stand out from others.
- secure new customers.
- secure repeat customers / business and build brand loyalty.
- maximise sales and market share.
- enable a higher price to be charged, thus, add value.
- provide marketing economies of scale.
- maximise profit / profit margins.
- increase the value of a business (*thus* ROI for shareholders).

Drawbacks / Limitations:

- Often requires high investment in **advertising** and **packaging**.
- Only successful if product lives up to expectations and image built through advertising.
- Bad press with one product can negatively affect the image, thus sales of other products with same brand name.

Merchandising: *Involves making decisions over:*

- ordering.
- what stock should be given prominence on display.
- where stock should be placed / positioned in store.
- how much space to allocate items to be promoted.
- how to display items to be promoted, incl. equipment / materials to use, and information to include.
- ambience eg appropriate lighting, music, enticing smells.

Benefits: Can stimulate impulse purchases, *thus* increase average spend, useful in supporting ad campaigns & sales promotions.

Drawbacks: Not effective in building customer loyalty, materials used can add to visual clutter - make areas look untidy.

Sales Promotions:

Types:

- **Into the pipeline** methods (aimed at intermediaries) eg discounts for bulk purchases, free merchandising / display material, better credit terms.
- **Out of the pipeline** methods (aimed at end-customer / consumer), eg free offers / gifts / samples, bonus packs (50% extra), multibuys (buy 1 get 1 free), money off coupons, reward cards, competitions, charity donations.

Benefits:

- Stimulate interest, create excitement about a product.
- Effective in producing immediate short-term sales results.
- Help achieve a wide range of objectives...

In B2C markets:	In B2B markets:
- encourage sales. - increase frequency of usage / purchase - increase off peak / season sales. - encourage sales of slow moving lines.	- obtain shelf space. - develop goodwill. - encourage retailers to promote the product. - encourage salesforce to push the product. - help salesforce to do their job. - increase distribution network. - push sales of slow moving lines.

Drawbacks:

- Can be expensive.
- Reduce price paid, *thus* reduce margins.
- Can tarnish quality image if used frequently.
- Not found effective in building long-term customer / brand loyalty.

Personal Selling:

Key Activities:

- Obtaining / making deliveries.
- Staffing exhibitions, giving talks / presentations / demonstrations.
- Giving free trials / samples.
- Offering advice, guidance.

Attendance at exhibitions and trade fairs provide a chance to:
- show how product works.
- test consumers reaction before release onto market.
- answer specific queries.
- attract free press coverage.

Salesperson usually involved in 6 key stages: Prospecting, Pre-approach, Approach, Presentation, Close, Follow-up.

Successful selling requires: Interpersonal skills, knowledge, faith, and confidence in the product, energy, determination, high self-motivation, pleasant appearance.

Benefits and Drawbacks:

Can be time consuming and expensive way to promote products to potential customers, resulting in high cost per contact / prospect. *However,* there is scope to:

- precisely target potential customers.
- hold the attention of the potential customer (prospect).
- obtain immediate feedback.
- tailor presentations / conversations to needs of customer.
- answer any queries, get immediate action, close sales.

May be essential for **complex products** and **high value purchases** eg houses, cars – when customers need advice and reassurance from an expert. Especially common in B2B marketing, and marketing of consumer durables.

Direct Marketing:

Direct Mail:
Promotional material sent to existing or potential customers by post

Benefits:
- Highly targeted and personalised.
- Higher response rate than advertising.
- No limit to length, scope for originality / total control over presentation.
- Hidden from competitors.
- Effectiveness easily measured.

Drawbacks:
- Considered junk mail by many, invasion of privacy - can tarnish image / reputation.
- Success depends on quality of mailing list - obtaining / maintaining up-to-date lists can be time consuming, expensive.
- Limited impact - no movement or sound.
- Relatively long lead time between design to mailing out promotional materials.

Door to Door Leaflet Marketing:

Promotional material dropped through potential customers' letter boxes.

Benefits & Drawbacks: Advantages of direct mail, but costs less. *However,* may not be as targeted and not personalised - more likely to be considered junk, *thus* response rate lower, although may still be higher than some forms of advertising. Impact also limited - with no movement or sound.

Telemarketing:
Salesperson (or recorded voice) solicits prospective customers over the phone.

Benefits:
- Highly targeted and personalised.
- Two-way communication, *thus*... immediate feedback, scope to tailor info to customer needs, answer queries.
- Can obtain immediate action, close sales.
- Response rates higher than advertising.
- Effectiveness easily measured.
- Wide reach and more prospects than personal selling - cost effective way to increase customer base geographically.
- Hidden from competitors.

Drawbacks:
- Unless highly targeted – seen as annoyance, invasion of privacy – can tarnish firm's image.
- Cost of obtaining up to date, accurate lists of potential customers can be high in relation to no. of sales gained.
- More people using technology to screen out unwanted calls from telemarketers - being backed by government legislation.

Email Marketing:
Uses electronic mail to send promotional messages to existing or potential customers.

Benefits:
- Global reach with little effort.
- Highly targeted and personalised.
- Costs much less, *thus* more affordable than many other forms of promotion.
- Very short lead time & instant delivery.
- Can obtain immediate response.
- Effectiveness easily tracked.
- Environmentally friendly.

Drawbacks:
- Difficulty in delivering messages (blocked).
- Content may not be displayed as intended.

Text Message Marketing:

Benefits:
- Highly targeted and personalised.
- Response rates higher than advertising.
- Messages cheap and easy to prepare.
- Relatively cheap to deliver / send.
- Short lead time & almost instant delivery.
- More likely to be read than email.
- Hidden from competitors.
- Effectiveness easily measured.

Drawbacks: Message has to be concise - limits how creative the content can be.

© APT Initiatives Ltd, 2011

Advertising:

Business Directories eg Yellow Pages:

Advantages:
- Wide reach, permanent basis.
- Basic listing free.
- Can track eg with separate phone line.

Disadvantages:
- Easily lost amongst other listings - unless large advert, which is costly.
- More consumers using online directories.
- Only updated annually.
- Limited colour, no movement or sound.
- On own very passive way to advertise.

Newspapers:

Advantages:
- Widely read - large audience.
- Scope to target geographic, demographic.
- Frequent publication + short lead time - change ad in light of changes in market.
- Reader can refer back (to advert).
- Relatively cheap (compared to TV).

Disadvantages: Low impact, response as:
- Limited colour, no movement or sound.
- Reproduction / layout can be poor.
- Many adverts lost amongst others.
- Short life and daily advert adds to costs.

Magazines:

Advantages:
- Scope to target those likely to be interested on national basis.
- Moderate life, read at leisure - more chance of advert being seen.
- Better reproduction and full colour advertisements (unlike newspapers).

Disadvantages:
- Higher cost than newspaper.
- Less frequent publication, longer lead time - message may become out of date.
- Lower impact (than TV, cinema).
- Slower response rate (than newspapers) - due to long lead time, moderate life.

TV:

Advantages:
- Wide reach, thus low cost per exposure.
- Can target geographic, demographic and psychographic segments.
- Greater impact (than print or radio).

Disadvantages:
- Limited length of exposure.
- Preferred ad times often sold out.
- Short-lived message - cannot refer back.
- Relatively expensive - air time, creation.
- Often not watched - annoying break.

Radio:

Advantages:
- Wide reach.
- Can target geographic, demographic and psychographic segments.
- Greater impact than print – sound / voices.

Disadvantages:
- Cannot refer back (until replayed).
- May not be listened to - listener's attention limited - often doing other things.
- Lower impact (than TV, cinema).

Cinema:

Advantages:
- Can target demographic, geographic.
- Captive audience.
- Higher impact (than print or radio) - colour, movement _and_ sound.

Disadvantages:
- Limited audience and mainly young.
- Message may only be seen once.

Poster: Can target geographic segments. **Billboards** – Repeatedly seen 24 hrs, _but_ rarely attract full attention - often driving, so message must be short & simple, may be considered traffic hazard, also affected by weather and graffiti. **Inside or outside public transport:** Low cost (c/w billboards). Inside: Captive audience - likely to be seen; Outside - distractions prevent full attention, _but_ wider, more diverse audience reach.

Internet Advertising:

Advantages over traditional advertising:

- Global reach.
- High accessibility / permanence.
- High targeting potential.
- Effectiveness easily measured.
- Easy to administer and instant updates.
- High impact.
- Low cost / Affordability.

Problems as promotional tool:

- Not everyone has access / easy access.
- Possible technical problems.
- Mechanical faults, power cuts.

Company Website:

Design cost, maintenance cost, web hosting fee.
However, potential benefits outweigh costs:

- Inexpensive way to reach customers across world.
- Reduces / eliminates need for paper-based sales / promotional materials.
- Information easily and instantly updated.
- Minimises labour admin costs – can display key company information, including FAQ's.
- Effectiveness can easily be measured.

However… On own, website will do little to gain business. Needs to be supported with other promotion or internet advertising effective in generating traffic to the site…

Search Engine Optimisation & Listings:

To maximise chance search on search engine (eg Google) will bring up website – use of descriptive titles and accurate 'meta tags'. Business can also pay for ads to appear on search engine results page. Usually charged 'per click' on advert. Can set a limit eg £5, £20, £100 per day, week, etc - once reached stops ad being displayed.

Free Link Exchanges and Affiliate Marketing:

Free links from related website to business's website, in exchange for link from business's website. Alternatively, selling business charged fee on every sale made from link – 'affiliate marketing' eg Amazon.

Links can help to increase business's ranking with search engines. *However,* visitors may be sidetracked into leaving the business's website via exchange link and not return.

Free or Paid Listings in Online Directories:

Similar benefits / drawbacks to directory listings in printed media. Additional benefit - listings can contain **hypertext link**, which user can click on and go straight to business's website for further information.

Social Network Advertising:

Can advertise to **consumers** on sites such as Facebook, MySpace, Twitter. Also sites such as LinkedIn, PartnerUp, Ryze - created to advertise, connect or create links with **other businesses**. Business creates profile pages users can choose to join, and be kept updated and informed. Paid advertising options work in similar way to major search engines, and based on 'pay per click' system.

Establishing presence on such sites is a fast, relatively cheap and easy way to make regular contact with **existing** customers, thus build customer relationships / loyalty, as well as to reach and gain **new** customers – as friends, family, other business professionals connected to the customers connected to the business's website can also view information about the business. Overall, a **highly cost effective way of increasing leads and generating sales.**

Influences on the Choice of Promotional Mix

Relative Extent to which Promotional Method is Likely to Reach & Obtain a Response from Target Market *eg:*

- Direct mail - more targeted than newspaper advertising.
- Personal selling - more effective at persuading customers to buy than advertising in general, *but* might only reach a few target customers at any time, compared to TV or national newspaper.
- Sales promotions - effective in encouraging response, but need another form of promotion to make target market aware they exist.
- Magazines - more effective in reaching defined segment than national newspaper and in getting a response - as use of colour - greater impact, in circulation longer - more likely to be seen.

Nature of the Target Market, Size & Location *eg:*

- Personal selling - large role in B2B marketing - as highly effective and more affordable as fewer people involved.
- Advertising - greater role in consumer (particularly mass) markets - where large no. and more diverse customers makes personal selling expensive.

Relative Cost & Availability of Finance / Budget

eg: National TV ad campaign may be too expensive for small business with limited funds.

Competitor Activities

eg: Special offer introduced by rival could lose business sales, unless business offers similar offer, or invests in branding to make product look superior.

Product Life Cycle *eg:*

- Launch and growth: PR, advertising, sales promotions effective to generate awareness, encourage purchase.
- Maturity: Emphasis on branding and packaging - to maintain market share.

Nature of the Product

eg: If use / benefits fairly obvious / simple to understand, personal selling unnecessary waste of resources – more appropriate for complex, technical products to fully explain, demonstrate, answer specific enquiries. If seasonal product eg ice cream, holidays in UK, then sales promotions effective to boost sales off-peak.

Legislation

eg: Due to health problems from use of tobacco, legislation over last 30 + years gradually restricted advertising and forced tobacco firms to use other elements of the mix – now largely limited to merchandising.

Findings from Market Research

Helps determine most appropriate mediums and messages to use to reach target market and persuade them to buy. New business might be able to obtain national statistics relating to 'leisure activities' eg what newspaper customers read, how often go to cinema etc, free of charge, from government reports such as Social Trends.

Business Objectives *eg:*

- Sales maximisation - use of sales promotions, packaging and merchandising to highlight special offers.
- changing image eg to one of social responsibility - sponsorship (of good causes), PR and advertising effective.

USING THE MARKETING MIX: PRICING

Price and Influences on Pricing Decisions

Significance of Price:

Directly influences:

- purchasing decision.
- overall demand.
- profitability.

Influences on Price:

Costs.

Customer **perceptions** re value.

Customers' **income**.

Availability / price of **substitutes**.

Other parts of mix - the more unique, the higher the price, promotion can increase perceived worth, intermediaries need return.

Position in **life cycle**.

Business **aims/objectives** eg upmarket image - high price, but high price risks low sales, market share.

Price **elasticity** of demand.

Price elasticity of demand:
a measurement of the extent to which demand for a particular product (or service) changes in response to a change in price; calculated by dividing % change in Qty demanded by % change in price.

Understanding & Using PED:

Price **elastic** product - **greater** than 1 - % change in D, greater than % change in price - customers **price-sensitive**. Elasticity **less** than 1 - product price **inelastic** - demand / customers **price-insensitive**.

Determinants:

Extent to which product regarded as necessity, or habit forming. If essential for survival eg food, or habit forming eg drugs, demand unlikely to be affected by change in price - price inelastic. Luxuries eg holidays more likely to be price elastic.

Availability of substitutes ie similar products. The greater the availability of close substitutes, the more elastic demand.

Price of product as proportion of income. If costs a small proportion of income eg sweets, car wash - less sensitive to changes in price (price inelastic) c/w product that costs a large proportion eg car, family holiday.

Calculation:
Firm reduces price from £20 to £16. Demand increases from 12,000 to 18,000 units. In % terms, price decreased by 20% (£4 / £20 X 100), demand increased by 50% (6,000 / 12,000 X 100). *Thus* PED (coefficient) is 2.5 (50% / 20%). For every 1% change in price, demand is likely to change by 2.5%.

Significance and Effect on Revenue:

Cutting price on price **elastic** product will **increase total revenue**. Eg: *Product has PED of 2.5. Selling price per unit £20, demand at this price 12,000 units, which generates sales revenue of £240,000. What will be the effect on revenue if price is reduced by 20% to £16?*

PED 2.5 = every 1% change in price, demand changes 2.5%, price reduced demand increases, price rises demand falls. *Thus*, if price reduced by 20%, demand rises 2.5 x 20% ie 50% ie 6,000 (12000 x 0.5) to 18000 units. Revenue at lower price will be **£280,000** (18000 x £16) ie **+£40,000**. NB might not lead to increased total profit - will also increase costs as more produced. To fully assess impact on profits, info on costs required.

Knowledge of PED can help forecast effect on sales of price changes, decide whether price change wise, as well help operations plan future output and organise resources (material, staffing), etc required.

Problems of Measurement:
Can be difficult and costly to obtain the info required to determine PED, especially as demand can be affected by a no. of variables at the same time, and it can be difficult to isolate variables.

© APT Initiatives Ltd, 2011

Pricing Strategies

Pricing strategies: courses of action relating to the selling price required to achieve a business's marketing objectives.

Price skimming: selling a new (or much improved version of a product) at a high price for a relatively short period of time.

Penetration pricing: selling a new product at a low price in order to gain a foothold in the market.

Price leaders: usually large businesses with large market share that set prices for products that are followed by other, usually smaller firms.

Price takers: usually small (independent) businesses that tend to set prices at the same level as those set by other, usually larger firms.

Predatory (or destroyer) pricing: setting a price at such a low level with a view to forcing rival firms out of the market.

Cost-plus pricing: setting prices by calculating the cost of producing the product and adding on a percentage (profit).

Full-cost pricing: setting the price for a product by calculating the average costs (fixed and variable, or direct and indirect) of producing the product, and adding a mark-up (percentage) for profit.

Mark-up: the percentage of the cost involved in producing a product that is added on to the cost in order to find the selling price.

Variable cost-plus pricing (or **direct cost-plus pricing**): setting the price of a product to cover all variable (or direct) costs plus a percentage mark-up as a contribution towards fixed (or indirect) costs and profit.

Customer value pricing: setting prices based on customers' perceived value of what the product is worth to them.

Price discrimination: offering the same or similar product at different prices, according to customer, place, or time.

Target based pricing: setting or adjusting prices in order to achieve specific targets, eg relating to sales volume or value, or profit.

Pricing Strategies Generally Associated with New Product Pricing

Price Skimming:

Main aim / focus (in the short-term) is to maximise sales revenues and profit as opposed to volume, market share. Dependent upon demand being price inelastic. Common to unique, innovative products eg fashion, toys, computer software, medicines.

Potential Benefits	Risks / Potential Drawbacks
Can help to… • recover R&D and product launch costs more quickly. • maximise profits. • build up high quality image.	• High prices attract competitors. • May make it easier for competitor to launch at lower price. • Failing to maximise sales volumes early on may result in not being able to hold the market share required to stay profitable when competition enters.

Penetration Pricing:

Main aim / focus is on sales volumes and market share, as opposed to revenue and profit – to encourage people to try the product and secure brand loyalty. The hope is that once established, price can be increased, or the business can enjoy higher profits from economies of scale. Dependent upon demand being price elastic. Common to mass markets, eg biscuits, confectionery, washing powder, crisps.

Potential Benefits	Risks / Potential Drawbacks
Can… • reduce unit costs - as a result of economies of scale from larger sales volumes. • maximise capacity utilisation. • discourage new competition - low price acts as 'barrier to entry'.	• Lower profit margins - need to be sustained long enough for strategy to be effective in gaining market share. • Low price can be associated with low quality. • Much harder to raise price later than reduce it. • Competitors may follow suit and reduce prices - unless product is seen as superior in some way, this will negate any sales advantage.

Cost-plus Pricing Strategies

Variable-cost Pricing:

Determine unit variable cost, add % mark-up - contribution towards fixed costs and profit. In short-run, as long as firm can pay variable costs it can survive. In long run, needs to cover total costs. *Eg:* Firm produces 18,000 units. VC are £63,000. FC are £190,000. Lowest price it can charge to survive in the: a) short-term? b) long-term?
a) £63,000 / 18,000 = £3.50 to cover variable costs.
b) £153,000 / 18,000 = £8.50 assuming costs + output stay the same.

Advantages:

- Simpler and quicker than full-cost pricing.

Risks / Drawbacks:

- Without detailed consideration of FC and accurate projection of likely demand, there is the risk of profit not being made.

Full-cost Pricing:

Set projected output, calculate total cost per unit, and add agreed profit margin. NB Fixed costs allocated on logical basis eg rent on factory floor space occupied by product. *Eg:* Firm produces 12,000 items at total cost of £21,000. Average cost = £1.75. Mark-up of 20% means each item sold at £2.10.

Advantages: *Ensures…*

- revenue will cover all costs and profit will be made.
- cost increases passed to customer - margins protected.

Weaknesses / Limitations:

- Assumes all units will be sold.
- FC per unit can only be estimated accurately if demand can accurately be predicted.
- Used in isolation, ignores price customers prepared to pay.
- Can only be used where no effective competition – rare.

Competitor-based Pricing Strategies

Price Leaders / Price Leadership:
Only possible if price leader's product is perceived to be the best by target market, ie there is little effective competition.

Price Takers / Going Rate Pricing:
Common to mass markets / highly competitive markets where there is low product differentiation, thus any increase in price is likely to result in customers going elsewhere.

Predatory / Destroyer Pricing:
If existing / new competitor(s) cannot match / sustain the lower price, they may lose customers and go out of business, or choose not to enter a market. The 'predator' then has fewer competitors, thus, increased sales and market share. Main drawback **profit sacrificed** in short-term. Common to competitive markets dominated by a few large firms (oligopoly). Against 'anti-competitive' legislation, but hard to prove.

Customer-based Pricing

Customer Value Pricing: The more beneficial customers view the product in relation to others, the higher the price they will pay, but this is also influenced by their disposable income. CVP can help **maximise sales revenues**, but finding out the value customers place on products and prices they are prepared to pay can be **time consuming & costly**.

Price Discrimination: Eg transport can be cheaper for OAPs, students (age), cheaper off peak (time). PD can maximise **revenue & profit**, highly effective for seasonal business to **maximising sales & capacity utilisation** off peak times. *But*, it can lead to **resentment** amongst customers paying full price.

In practice most firms use an element of cost <u>and</u> market (ie competition and customer-based) pricing.

Pricing Tactics:

Pricing tactics: measures taken to achieve short-term objectives or respond to particular situations in the short-term.

Loss leaders: products with very low prices that are used to attract customers to buy other, more fully priced products.

Psychological pricing: setting prices at a level that creates an illusion amongst customers about the price, or an impression about the value of the product they are purchasing.

Psychological Pricing: Previously associated with setting prices just below whole number eg £2.99, £2.98, £2.95 instead of £3.00 - to make product seem cheaper. Associated with bargain or no-frills. economy products. Setting prices at the whole number ie at £10 instead of £9.99 may now help to convey quality.

Loss Leaders: Commonly used by supermarkets - customers encouraged through doors by pricing product(s) at very low level - may not even cover costs. The hope is that they will spend money on other, more profitable items, which will more than offset any losses on the loss leader. Loss leader is carefully placed so customers pass many other products before they reach it. Relies on impulse buying.

Other Pricing tactics: **Special Offer Pricing** eg 3 for 2, 50p off coupon; **Discounting** eg for payments by cash, early payment, bulk purchases, or to sell off old stock (clothes).

USING THE MARKETING MIX: PLACE
Types of Distribution Channel, Outlets / Distributors

Distribution channel: the different ways in which a business's product is made available to the end-customer / consumer.

Distributors: businesses involved in the process of making a product available to the end-customer or consumer (user).

Direct Sales / Selling: does not involve the use of intermediaries such as wholesalers, retailers, or agents to sell a business's product to the end-customer or consumer (user).

Retailers: businesses who buy from wholesalers or direct from producers for sale to the public in shops or other retail outlets.

Wholesalers: businesses who buy large quantities of goods from producers or agents acting on behalf of producers, for resale in smaller quantities to retailers or other business users.

Agents: independent people or businesses contracted to negotiate sales and handle the distribution of a product on behalf of the seller.

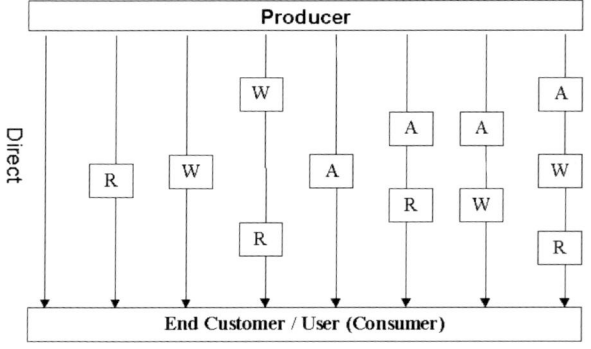

In some cases the product goes straight from the producer to the end-customer / consumer. In other cases intermediaries eg wholesalers (W), retailers (R) and / or agents (A) are used.

Direct Sales:

Can take various forms. May involve…

- sales representatives - personal selling.
- direct mail incl. the use of catalogues.
- other direct marketing eg telesales, email marketing, text messaging.
- website with online ordering facilities.

Potential Advantages	Potential Disadvantages
• May enable a firm to sell at a lower price, thus, enjoy greater sales, and / or higher profits. • Close contact with end-customer, thus, may be able to respond more quickly to changing needs. • Cash flow - payment likely to be made at the time the goods are received.	• Requires considerable marketing effort - can take focus away from production. • Can significantly increase administration, stockholding and distribution costs.

Selling via website with online ordering facilities:

Benefits	Drawbacks
For the Business: • Access to global market w/o fixed costs or risk involved in physically opening more outlets - rapid expansion possible. • No opening / closing hours - orders placed any time of day. • Minimum cost to handle and process orders - automated. • FAQ's + areas for customer feedback, enquiries, requests, etc - helps cut labour costs and enhance the service provided. • Invoices and receipts can also be sent via email - reducing stationery, printing costs. • Overall, can be more profitable or competitive - as lower prices may be charged due to lower costs. *For the Customer:* • Rapid, convenient service - order any time of day w/o leaving home (or workplace). • Potentially lower prices - as a result of lower overheads.	• Cost to design, maintain, update site, (but small c/w sales). • Cost of processing payments - requires merchant account / online secure payment service provider - take fee (% of the sale). • Some customers lack trust in security and confidentiality of online transactions - fear of internet fraud, identity theft. • Some customers lack skills or confidence to buy online. • Lack of physical contact with products prior to purchase may discourage some people from buying. • No personal interaction - some people might prefer human contact. • Online purchases do not immediately satisfy need or desire - customers have to wait delivery through 'snail mail' (24 hrs +). • Not everyone has easy access to computers. • Potential for delays and lost info from mechanical faults / breakdowns / power cuts.

Selling through Retailers:

Traditional (as opposed to online) retailers often locate near where people live - easy access. Often advertise and provide feedback to producers on customer demand / reaction to products. Add on profit margin to price paid to producer (wholesale) before selling to end-customer. Also provide advice, after sales service, credit facilities to consumer.

Potential Advantages	Potential Disadvantages
• Can be a highly cost-effective way to reach a large and dispersed market. • Traditional retailer overcomes problems that restrict online sales eg access, trust, confidence, preference to touch products before buying. • Assist in promotion, allow producer to concentrate on production, rather than marketing.	• Less control over price end-customer pays. • Potentially lower margins. • May require considerable promotional effort - competition for shelf space can be high. • Major retailers have considerable power - can impose conditions over quality, delivery, price - lower margins. • Retailers likely to buy on credit - can use power to insist on lengthy credit - negative effect on cash flow.

Selling through Wholesalers:

Will store goods until required by retailers and regularly deliver goods to retailer. May even pack and brand goods for producers or large retailers. Add on profit margin to price paid to producer before selling the product on.

Potential Advantages	Potential Disadvantages
• Can be highly cost-effective way for producers to reach large and dispersed market. • Allows producer to focus on production not marketing. • Reduces need for producer or retailer to carry large stocks – wholesaler provides storage facilities.	• Wholesaler may not put as much effort into promoting the product. • Price end-customer pays increases as wholesaler adds on own margin.

Selling through Agents:

Agent usually adds mark-up or earns commission on each sale. Widely used in importing / exporting.

Potential Advantages	Potential Disadvantages
• Reduced distribution costs, marketing effort and risk – allows producer to concentrate on production. • Agents often have expert knowledge, contacts - manufacturers may lack finance and resources (eg time, know-how, contacts, money) to sell abroad).	• Agent of several products may not give product sufficient attention if others more profitable. • Like all intermediaries, can create barriers between producer and consumer - restrict direct feedback, less power over end-price.

Physical Transportation Considerations

Q's to consider/ Factors Influencing Choice		Advantages	Disadvantages
What mode(s) of transport should be used? What are the best possible routes? Use own fleet or hire outside carriers? How can safe delivery of the goods be ensured?	Road	• Door to door delivery - unless overseas locations involved, in which case other forms of transport eg air / sea also required.	• Subject to traffic delays, especially in bad weather. • Slower than rail over long distances. • Can only carry relatively small loads.
	Rail	• Less subject to delays in adverse weather. • Cheap and quick over long distances. • Can transport large and heavy loads.	• May not be able to reach far away places. • No door to door service.
	Sea	• Fully loaded lorries can be transported. • Generally cheaper than air.	• Slow. • Still requires other forms of transport.
	Air	• Extremely rapid. • Can be more cost effective over long distances. • Provides greater security for expensive items.	• Not appropriate for bulky goods. • More prone to delays in adverse weather. • Still needs to be linked to other forms of transport.

© APT Initiatives Ltd, 2011

Factors Influencing Choice of Distribution Channel, Outlet / Distributor

Costs

In some cases, might not be cost effective for producer to sell direct to end-customer / consumer

Size & Spread of the Market, *eg:*

- If market large and dispersed - long channel may be required, with many intermediaries and various modes of transport.

- If market small - may be possible to distribute product directly to individual consumers.

Size of Producer *eg the larger...*

- the more resources they are likely to have available to set up own networks.

- the more they may be able to take advantages of economies of scale through purchasing own vehicles.

Ability & Experience of Producer

Intermediaries used when producers lack ability or experience in marketing. *Thus*, more likely to be used when starting out.

Nature of the Product *eg direct / short channels appropriate for:*

- **Bulky** products - as handling costs likely to be higher.
- **Fragile** - to limit handling, chance of breakages.
- **Perishable** - to limit chance of going past shelf-life.
- **Tailor made products** - to ensure consumers' needs met.
- **Technically complex** - to allow explanations, questions, answers to specific queries.

NB Services usually sold direct (excluding package holidays).

Needs of Customer re: volume, frequency, urgency, value, *eg:*

- Next day delivery needed for lowest possible price - quickest and most cost-effective method.

- If customers buy large amounts infrequently - short, direct channel may be possible.

Desired Degree of Control:

Once product sold on to intermediary, intermediary assumes control over the way product is marketed ie how it is priced, described, displayed. Producer may wish to retain control and protect its reputation.

Reputation of Intermediaries & Attitude Towards Product

If difficulty securing suitable intermediaries ie reliable, efficient, sufficiently interested in the business's product to invest necessary time and effort in 'selling' it to customers, then direct channels may be the most effective option in maximising sales.

Competitors

What are they offering?

Can this be matched in terms of delivery times and quantity?

Legal Restrictions

eg: Certain drugs can only be sold by pharmacists through prescription; alcohol requires a licence.

Technology

Eg: Internet enabled firms to reach global marketplace relatively cost effectively, w/o intermediaries.

MARKETING AND COMPETITIVENESS
Possible Impacts of Market Conditions and Degree of Competition

Market conditions: characteristics of a market such as level and intensity of competition, barriers to entry, rate of market growth.

Competitors: other firms operating in the same market and providing a similar product or service.

Degree of competition: the quantity and intensity (eg strength, concentration and power) of businesses operating in the same market that provide the same or similar product or service.

Market structures: concern the number and relative strength of buyers and sellers, as well as other factors including the extent of product differentiation, and ease of entry into and exit out of a market. There are four basic types: perfect competition, monopoly, monopolistic competition and oligopoly.

Perfect competition: where many firms sell an identical product that have no control over price.

Monopoly: where there is one large firm selling a product with no close substitutes that has considerable control over prices and supply.

Oligopoly: where a small number of large firms sell similar products that have some control over price.

Monopolistic competition: where there are a large number of small firms selling differentiated products that have some control over price.

Barriers to entry: market conditions that make it difficult or expensive to enter such as economies of scale, technological capability required to compete effectively, high start-up costs, legal protection of property including intellectual property acquired by businesses already operating within the market.

Barriers to exit: market conditions that make it difficult or expensive to leave eg high liquidation costs.

Other Terms Used to Describe Markets:

- **Fragmented:** consist of large no. of small sellers or buyers.
- **Growing:** showing increase in demand over time.
- **Emerging:** in process of rapid growth & industrialisation.
- **Stagnated:** showing little growth.
- **Mature:** lacking significant growth or innovation.
- **Saturated:** where almost every customer has product.
- **Declining:** where annual revenues are falling steadily.

Impact of Competition

Forces firms to look more carefully at how they can meet / exceed customer requirements, eg by lowering prices, improving quality, issuing incentives eg free gifts.

Encourages firms to be **efficient** and **reduce costs** to enable lower prices.

Porter's 5 Forces Model:
Concern microenvironment - affect firm's ability to serve its customers and make a profit - consist of:

- **bargaining power of suppliers.**
- **bargaining power of buyers** (customers).
- **threat of substitutes** (rival products / services).
- **threat of new entrants** (barriers to entry).
- **degree of rivalry** (intensity of competition).

Used to understand factors affecting the industry within which firm operates, help decisions over how to improve competitiveness.

Market conditions and degree of competition not only influence **tactical** decisions over elements of the marketing mix, but also **major strategic decisions** over whether it is worth the time, effort, cost, and risk involved in entering a particular market.

Perfect Competition

Key Characteristics

- Many sellers, many buyers.
- Each relatively small.
- Identical product.
- Perfect information.
- Buyers can easily switch.
- Buyers have no personal preferences / loyalties, *thus...*
- Demand is perfectly elastic.
- No barriers to entry / exit.

NB 'ideal' – in practice no markets are perfectly competitive.

Examples (that come close)

- Large fish, fruit & veg markets.
- Stock market.

Possible Impacts

Sellers:

- compete on price alone.
- have little power - price takers.
- may enjoy high (excess) profits in short-run, competed away in long-run as firms freely enter.
- strive for efficiency, cut costs - as firms enter - to lower prices.

Consumers:

- Large choice, low prices.
- Little time, effort to gather info to buy - as products identical.

Monopoly

Key Characteristics

- One firm supplying market.
- No close substitutes.
- Relatively inelastic demand.
- Very high barriers to entry.

Examples

- Royal mail - letter delivery.
- Microsoft (near monopoly) - PC operating systems.

Possible Impacts

Monopolist:

- has considerable power over price - price maker.
- may attempt to raise prices to enjoy high profits.
- may use price discrimination to gain more profit.
- is more able to benefit from economies – higher profits.
- is under less pressure to keep costs and prices down.

Consumers:

- Less choice.
- Higher prices. *But...*
- little time, effort required to gather info to help make purchasing decisions.

Monopolistic Competition

Key Characteristics

- Many buyers, many sellers.
- Each seller small share.
- Differentiated product, but not sufficient to eliminate products as substitutes.
- Few barriers to entry / exit.

Examples

- Cereal manufacturers.
- Café's & restaurants.
- Clothes retailers.
- Hairdressers.
- Electricians, plumbers.
- Insurance companies.

Possible Impacts

Sellers:

- have some control over price - as differentiated product + many small sellers - free to set prices as if monopoly.
- use non price elements eg adverts to win sales, convince customers to pay more.
- less pressure to cut costs.

Consumers:

- Can be time consuming, costly to gather info required to make purchasing decisions.

Oligopoly

Key Characteristics

- Small no. of large sellers have majority market share.
- Mutually interdependent - one seller changes price, others likely to follow.
- Differentiated product, *but* close substitutes, *thus* demand is price elastic.
- High barriers to entry.

Examples

- Groceries (supermarkets).
- Finance (banks).
- Motor vehicle manufacture.
- Petrol (petrol stations).

Possible Impacts

Sellers:

- have considerable market power - price setters.
- need to consider responses / counter responses of other main sellers in decisions.
- can enjoy high profits in long-run - as high barriers (eg economies of scale, expensive ad campaigns) prevent new entrants capturing 'excess' profits.

Determinants of Competitiveness

Competitiveness: refers to the ability of an individual business to win customers over rivals. It involves the ability to give the customer something over and above rivals that customers value eg lower prices, superior product / service quality, faster delivery of product / service.

Competitive advantage: something that places a business above its rivals, eg the ability to offer a superior product / service or lower prices.

Determinants of competitiveness: factors influencing a business's ability to be competitive, ie its ability to give customers something over and above rivals that customers value, such as a superior product / service, lower prices.

Forms of Competitive Advantage:

Lower prices.

Superior product eg lasts longer, more features/benefits - <u>actual</u> or *perceived*.

Superior delivery of product offering / higher levels of customer service eg faster delivery, more helpful staff.

General Determinants of Competitiveness:

The capabilities of the business - its resources / assets:

- material, human and capital resources.
- Knowledge, experience, and ability to learn.
- organisational culture.
- reputation, brands, intellectual property rights.

The business's ability to use its resources to gain competitive advantage. Involves taking into account:

- **External factors:** factors outside the firm's control - opportunities, threats arising in its environment eg changes in customer requirements, competitor activities, macro-economic factors eg changes in interest rates.
- **Internal factors:** factors under the firm's control / at its disposal – strengths, weaknesses eg relating to skills and productivity of the workforce, organisational culture.

A business should identify and utilise its internal strengths (core competencies) to take advantage of opportunities arising in its external environment.

Factors Influencing Ability to Offer Lower Prices:

Costs. The higher the costs in relation to competitors, the less able to offer lower prices. A business may seek to cut costs eg through **new technologies, training** and **incentives** to increase staff productivity.

Factors Influencing Ability to Offer Superior Product/Service:

- **Time and finance (made) available to undertake market research and R & D** – to identify what customers value, how to stand out from rivals, innovate accordingly.
- **Entrepreneurial skills of owners and managers**, as well as **skill levels of staff**, and **finance (made) available to invest in training** if required – to enable effective innovation to take place.
- **Organisational culture and structure** – where innovation is not stifled, management and staff are able to make timely response to changes in competitor activities, customer needs.
- **Ability of the product / service idea to be legally protected** eg through copyright, patents, trademarks – to prevent others copying.
- Business's **overall attitude and approach to quality** – influences ability to lower price (as a result of lower costs), as well as ability to offer a superior product / level of service.

© APT Initiatives Ltd, 2011

Methods of Improving Competitiveness

Forwards vertical integration: involves a business buying out or joining forces with one of its distributors.

Backwards vertical integration: involves a business buying out or joining forces with one of its suppliers.

Lean production: involves minimising the use of key business resources (ie materials, labour, capital, factory floor space, time), and eliminating waste *without* reducing customer value.

Streamlining: involves making a business more efficient by getting rid of non-essential aspects of the business.

Profit centres: units in a business that generate revenue and incur costs, and have their own income statement (profit & loss account).

Decentralisation: the process of passing authority and responsibility for decision-making downwards from the upper levels of management to people at lower levels in the organisation.

Matrix organisational structures: where staff are organised into project teams that consist of people involved in a particular function, as well as people involved in a particular product or customer group. Each employee reports to a functional or divisional manager and project manager.

Value analysis: a process that seeks to cut the costs of producing a product without reducing the 'value' of the product from the customer's perspective, and / or increasing the value of a particular product (in the eyes of the customer) without increasing the costs.

The AQA unit specification requires knowledge of **marketing** and **non-marketing** methods to increase competitiveness. The one set of methods directly relates to the other. *Eg:*

- **Reducing prices** can only be achieved by accepting smaller profits, or by **cutting costs.**
- Offering a product or level of service superior to rivals, may be achieved by **improving quality, staff training**.

Ultimately, the **rarer** the business's **resources**, the more **difficult** to **imitate**, and the more **capable** to **change** in response to changes in the external environment, the more likely a business will be able to sustain its competitiveness / competitive advantage.

Marketing Methods:

- **Lowering prices** - unless accompanied by cost reduction lowers margins.
- **Improving the product / service** to provide greater benefits eg extra features, better performance, appearance, after sales service.
- Making the product / service **appear superior** - through **promotion**.
- Making the product / service **more easily accessible** - eg available at more locations, more convenient times.
- **Market** (customer and competitor) **research** and a **market orientation** - improvements must be based on what customers value and competitors are doing.

Non-marketing Methods:

- **Source cheaper, or better quality, more reliable suppliers** and **invest time and effort in building solid relationships** – to reduce costs, thus lower prices, and / or improve product quality and / or responsiveness to changing customer needs.
- **Implement flexible working practices** eg use of temporary, part-time staff - to minimise labour costs, or use of homeworking / teleworking – to minimise floor space requirements, thus rental costs and business rates - enabling lower prices.
- **Outsource non-core / critical activities** – reduces wages and salaries - enabling lower prices.
- **Relocate to areas with access to lower-cost factors of production** eg cheaper rent, raw materials, labour - enabling lower prices.
- **Forward or backwards vertical integration** – to obtain materials at cost price / cut out the intermediary - enabling lower prices.
- **Invest in new technologies, machinery, equipment or new methods of production** – new technologies may enable products to perform better, or services to more closely meet customer needs. Automation can significantly cut costs - enabling lower prices, as well as improved quality / level of service. Use of CAD helps firms to invent products much more cheaply - enabling lower prices, as well as reach the market much more quickly, thus faster response to changing customer needs, and competitor activities.
- **Implement lean production techniques** eg cell production, just in time, simultaneous engineering, critical path analysis – minimise costs - enabling lower prices, as well as improve quality and reliability.
- **Maximise productivity and capacity utilisation** eg by training, incentives to increase motivation, planned, preventative maintenance, improvements in layout / arrangement of tasks – keeps fixed costs per unit to a minimum - enabling lower prices.
- **Invest in training** – minimises costs - enabling lower prices, and ensures high quality products / standards of customer service, as well as enables firm to be more responsive to changing market conditions / keep ahead of rivals.
- **Rationalise / Streamline** eg move to smaller premises, close down a particular factory / plant / outlet in a particular location, sell off surplus machinery, downsize, delayer – to reduce overheads, increase capacity utilisation - enabling lower prices.
- **Improve financial planning and control** – tight control of costs, thus lower prices, may be achieved through the use of profit centres, budgets, closer monitoring / supervision of labour and materials, incentives based on targets re: costs / cost reduction.
- **Improve organisational design / structure** eg through delayering, decentralisation, a matrix organisational structure – to increase responsiveness to changing customer needs, and ability to stay ahead of rivals.
- **Use value analysis** ie assess new / existing products according to function, aesthetics, economy of manufacture, and designs products to maximise customer value <u>and</u> minimise production costs - enabling lower prices.
- **Secure intellectual property rights** eg patents, trademarks – to protect ideas / knowledge that provides competitive advantage.
- **Build a 'Total Quality' culture** – maximises product / service quality <u>and</u> minimises costs - enabling lower prices.

MAXIMISING YOUR PERFORMANCE IN THE EXAMINATION

Summary of AQA GCE (AS/A) Level Business Studies Mark Schemes

All GCE (AS/A) Level Business Studies examinations test your ability to **use** your knowledge. The better you are at **using** your knowledge, the higher the mark awarded.

There are essentially 4 main skills an examiner looks for when deciding what marks to award you in your responses to examination questions. These consist of: **Knowledge and understanding, Application of knowledge, Analysis** and **Evaluation**. These four levels of ability are the four main assessment objectives (AO's) of AQA GCE (AS/A) Level Business Studies.

These skills can be ranked in ascending order of difficulty, with knowledge being the easiest skill to demonstrate, and evaluation the hardest. As you progress through your course, greater emphasis is placed on the demonstration of evaluation skills.

When the examiner reads your answer he / she looks for evidence of each the above skills / assessment objectives and makes decisions about how well you have demonstrated these skills. In general, you need to be able to demonstrate sound application, analysis and evaluation in order to secure high marks. However, it is not possible to evaluate, analyse or apply knowledge, without first having acquired knowledge. Consequently, knowledge is the foundation of all your answers.

The table adjacent relating to a question worth 15 marks should help you to understand the above points more clearly. Subsequent pages explain in detail what you need to do to demonstrate each of the four skills.

Level	Descriptor	
	Knowledge and Understanding, Application, Analysis (11 marks)	*Evaluation (4 marks)
L5	11-10 marks Good application **and** Good analysis	
L4	9-7 marks Good application **or** analysis **and** Limited application **or** analysis	
L3	6-4 marks Limited application **and** analysis **or** Good application **or** analysis	4-3 marks Candidate offers judgement plus full justification
L2	3-2 marks Knowledge **and / or** Weak application **or** analysis	2 marks Candidate offers judgement plus limited justification
L1	1 mark Limited knowledge	1 mark Candidate offers undeveloped judgement based on evidence

*Marks awarded for 'Evaluation' are also based on the quality of your written communication.

Note: The above table is based upon the most recent mark scheme for Unit 2 (BUSS2) published by the AQA examination board (at the time of writing), which differs to previous mark schemes used by the examination board following the publication of the new specification in 2008.

The table shows that if a question is worth 15 marks and you only demonstrate knowledge, with no application, analysis or evaluation, then you can only gain 1 mark. If you demonstrate application and analysis with no evaluation, then you can gain between 4 and 11 marks. The exact mark gained depends upon the extent to which you demonstrate each of these skills. NB Failure to demonstrate any of the above skills in relation to the question set, will gain zero marks.

Individual Assessment Objectives Explained

Knowledge and Understanding (AO1)

Demonstrating knowledge and understanding may include:

- **providing a definition of a key business term;**
- **describing a theory or part of a theory;**
- **providing an example;**
- **providing a simple explanation of the facts, without referring to specific evidence presented in the question or data response material.**

For example, in a question asking you to evaluate ways in which a particular business might secure the additional capacity it requires to meet demand at peak times, knowledge and understanding may be demonstrated by defining what capacity is (ie the maximum level of output a business can produce within a particular period of time eg a week, month, quarter, or year, with its present resources, eg premises, plant, machinery, equipment, and labour), and / or stating ways in which additional capacity might be secured to cope with demand at peak times **in general** eg use of overtime, temporary labour, hiring as opposed to buying any additional equipment required, use of shift work, or subcontracting work out to another business (outsourcing).

Demonstration of knowledge and understanding on its own will not enable you to achieve a pass.

Application of Knowledge and Understanding (AO2)

The ability to apply knowledge requires you to understand and appreciate the importance or significance of it, within the context provided for you in the question or data response material. Demonstrating application of knowledge involves:

- **developing points thoroughly with <u>specific reference to evidence presented</u> in the question / data response material.**

Following on from the capacity question above, to secure marks for application you would have to identify relevant methods to secure the additional capacity required at peak times for **the particular business in question** by referring to the evidence presented. Let us assume, for example, that the data response material informs us that the business in question currently operates a 5-day week, with staff working 9am to 5pm Monday to Friday. Stating the following would secure marks for application… *'In this particular case, the business operates a 5 day week with staff working 9am to 5pm each day of the week, and so additional capacity might be able to be secured by running shifts at evenings during the week and / or at weekends during peak times.'* NB Naming the business is not application; if the name can be replaced with another, without any change to the meaning of the answer, application has not been demonstrated.

Demonstration of application of knowledge and understanding only, will not earn higher than a D grade, and more likely a grade E.

© **APT Initiatives Ltd**, 2011

Analysis (AO3)

Analysis is about recognising and discussing relationships between different pieces of evidence and the possible causes or consequences of a particular aspect relating to the business or situation under review, by referring to some or all the evidence available.

You cannot analyse (or evaluate) without first acquiring knowledge and understanding. If, for example, you were asked to analyse or discuss methods of marketing a business might use to increase its competitiveness, you would first need to know what is meant by 'competitiveness', what are 'methods of marketing', and you would need to understand how marketing might improve a business's competitiveness in general, before you could answer the question.

To demonstrate analysis, you must **ensure that every point made is considered and explored in detail, including the possible <u>impact</u> on the business and <u>consequences</u> for the business of any problems or issues being considered, and / or solutions you are putting forward.** Depending precisely on how a question is phrased, you have opportunities to present negative and positive impacts and consequences, both in the short term and long term, and with regard to a business's various stakeholders. Marks for analysis are, in fact, often awarded for considering **more than one point of view.** However, simply listing advantages and disadvantages if already obvious from the data response material, will not secure marks for analysis. Your answers must **always go beyond what is already evident in the data you have been given to answer the question.** You must be **selective** and explain *why* something may be advantageous or disadvantageous for the business in question by taking into account, for example, the aims and objectives and influence and / or experience of the owners, shareholders and managers, as well as the business's markets, customers, suppliers, creditors, resources and economic climate, etc.

With reference to the question on capacity above, analysis would involve discussing the **<u>impact</u>** and the **<u>consequences</u>** of your suggestions to secure additional capacity **<u>for this particular business</u>**, always referring to any evidence provided about the business. For example, let us assume that the data response material also informs us that very few staff are willing to work overtime at peak times, even at higher rates of pay. You might, therefore, explain the following in relation to shift work... *'Running additional shifts in the evening and / or at weekends would help to **maximise the output** that could be produced from the current premises and existing machinery. However, because few staff are willing to work overtime, additional, temporary staff would need to be hired, and this would **incur extra recruitment** (unless agency staff were used), **induction / training and administration costs.*** This answer – in just two sentences – demonstrates analysis (and application). It **makes use of the information provided** in the data response material to consider the **impact** and **consequences** of a specific and relevant method that the business in question might be able to use to increase capacity at peak times. Further marks for analysis could also be gained by stating the following... *'Whether or not temporary labour was required, employees might expect to be paid a premium rate for working 'unsociable' hours that might be, say, between 1.2 to 1.6 times their usual hourly rate. Therefore, if premium rates were applied, evening and / or weekend working would **increase labour costs**. Labour costs would also increase if extra supervision was required to operate the additional shift(s). On the other hand, evening and / or weekend working could help to **reduce unit costs overall**, as a result of **greater capacity utilisation**, as well as **'off-peak' utility charges'**.*

Consistently demonstrating analysis, with some application of knowledge and understanding, is likely to secure a B, possibly, an A grade.

Evaluation (AO4)

Evaluation concerns actually **judging** which solutions you put forward are the best, or points you have made are the most relevant or significant, based exclusively on what has been analysed. Evaluation may be achieved by:

- **prioritising points / suggestions**, for example, by ranking them in time order, stating what should be done in the short term, and what in the long term, with reasons why;
- **assessing the extent to which your suggestions will work** and explaining **on what success any proposals you put forward may be based;**
- **assessing the degree of impact** based on alternative solutions.

All decisions should be **logical** and **balanced**. To ensure that they are you need to:

- **consider all the evidence presented** in the data response material and **more than one side to an argument.** There is often no 'one best way' and answers should recognise that there are a variety of responses to any situation and discuss all the alternatives.

- **explain the reasons behind preferred options,** which must be **related to evidence presented in** the question. With regard to this, the **suitability** and **feasibility** of any of your proposals / recommendations should take into account the following:

  - the nature of the business, its markets and activities;
  - the aims and objectives of the business;
  - its resources;
  - the objectives, power and activities of other key stakeholders, in particular, customers, competitors and owners / shareholders;
  - government policy and the economic climate
  - other external influences such as legislation.

A key point to recognise and emphasise with regard to evaluation is that information presented is often one-sided ie biased. Therefore, you must **look out for and be able to distinguish between fact and opinion.** Evidence that comes from an unreliable source, or is somewhat out of date should also be recognised in your judgements. Furthermore, all the information required to form a definitive conclusion is not always provided in the data response material. Therefore,

- **identifying what information is missing and explaining *why* it might be required, *how* it might be used, or *how* it might affect the assessment of a particular problem / issue / situation, or decision to be made, will demonstrate evaluation.**

Overall, you will need to make decisions between conflicting arguments, put forward your opinion based on evidence presented in the question / data response material, and justify your selection by weighing up the advantages and disadvantages of each alternative.

Key Words & Phrases to Build 'Higher Level' Answers

AO2: Application of Knowledge & Understanding

- In this case...
- This means that...
- Because...

AO3: Analysis

- Therefore...
- This will lead to...
- The effect of this is...
- This is likely to result in...
- However...
- On the other hand...
- The dis / advantages of this are...
- The consequences of this are...
- The impact of this is...
- If X happens then Y might occur, if A happens then B might occur

AO4: Evaluation

- Overall...
- On balance...
- In the short-term / long-term...
- The most likely cause is... because...
- The greatest effect that this will have on the business is... because...
- The most appropriate solution out of those discussed is... because...
- In these circumstances it is more likely / less likely that... because...
- This may be more / less important when... because...
- Whether this leads to... depends upon...
- Whether this works depends upon...
- The extent of the impact of this issue will depend upon...

Additional Phrases to Use in the Examination

Never be certain. There is often evidence missing and a range of external factors influencing the situation or business presented in the question that could change at any time, and influence the outcome. Therefore,

- avoid stating will, must, should, would, ought to, have to.
- use other less definite words and phrases such as **may, might, could, and it is possible that.**

© APT Initiatives Ltd, 2011

Command Words & Appropriate Responses

Not all questions at AS level provide scope for, or require, analytical and evaluative answers. It is important to be aware of the sort of answer the examiner is seeking. An obvious indicator is the number of marks allocated for a question (or part question). The other key indicator is the first few words or the 'command' word or phrase used in the question. Hence, the table below outlines the type of response required by the various command words or phrases that might be used in **AQA GCE AS Level questions.** The assessment objective required (ie AO1, AO2, AO3 and AO4) has also been identified. Knowledge of these will help to ensure that you do not over-run on questions not requiring analytical and evaluative answers, and preserve time for those that do.

QUESTION	RESPONSE	AO
What is meant by	Give a definition; describe the meaning of	1
Identify	Recognise and briefly describe	1
Calculate	Use the figures provided in the text to work something out	2
Explain	Make clear and give reasons for; clarify using examples	2
Analyse	Recognise and discuss relationships between different factors; identify and describe the cause and effect, impact and consequences of a particular situation, by referring to some or all the evidence available	3
Examine	Consider in depth; make a point and fully develop it	3
Discuss	Describe different aspects of the subject / present two sides of the argument, and give a reasoned conclusion	4
Evaluate	Judge or assess the likely worth / advantages / disadvantages / success, stating *why* - by referring to the evidence available	4
Justify	Give reasons to support an argument or action	4
Recommend	Consider the evidence and write down the course of action you consider to be the most appropriate, stating reasons why	4
To what extent	Determine how true something is, by explaining both sides to an argument and making a judgement	4

The Structure of the Examination Paper

Unit 2 is marked out of **80.** You have **1 hour 30 minutes** to answer the questions. All the questions are compulsory and are based on data response material.

You need to take care not to spend too much time on questions only worth a few marks and leave yourself short of time to complete questions requiring more extended responses, carrying high marks. Allowing some time to read through the paper and to read through your answers at the end (to check for any errors or omissions, and any grammatical errors) you have approximately **80 minutes** to answer all the questions. This equates to **1 minute per mark**. Therefore, for questions only worth 2 marks (eg *'Identify...'*) you should not take longer than 2 minutes to write your answer. For questions worth 11-15 marks (eg *'To what extent... Discuss... Justify your view'*), you should try to write your answer within 11-15 minutes.

Practicing doing questions in a set time limit is absolutely essential. Many students have the knowledge and ability to secure high grades but fail due to lack of time.

NB The mark schemes, structure and requirements of examination papers may change from time to time, and so it is important to check that the above information still applies since the publication of this book.

TOP TIPS TO MAXIMISE YOUR PERFORMANCE IN THE EXAMINATION

1. **Read** through the **entire question paper** at least **twice**.

2. Work out **approximate timings** for each question. This should be based on the number of marks per question and the total time allowed. With questions worth 11 or more marks, you must allow a few minutes to plan. **Planning** will help to keep your answers to the point, logical, and will help you to prioritise – all essential to secure high grades.

3. Answer the question you find the **easiest first.** This will help to build up your confidence.

4. **Read the question carefully.** Make sure you fully understand what you are being asked to do **before** you start writing.

5. For questions involving **calculations, always show your workings out.** Marks can be gained for using the correct formula / method of approach if the final answer is incorrect.

6. Treat every answer as discrete / self-contained, ie **do not refer the examiner back to points you have made in previous answers.** (This is especially relevant with the advent of on-line marking).

7. **Keep within the time allowed.** If you start to run over time on one question, stop and come back to it at the end. (Students often gain the most marks in the first part of their answer).

8. **Regularly read through your work,** not just at the end. Firstly, to check all points make sense and directly relate to the question set. (Many students, once they start writing, stray from the original question and this wastes valuable time). Secondly, to check for spelling, punctuation and grammatical areas – marks are awarded for quality of written communication.

9. If you think you've missed an important point out – **don't panic!** Mark where you want to make this point and direct the examiner to a relevant section at the end.

© APT Initiatives Ltd, 2011

For questions carrying high marks:

10. Think about your answer and, where relevant, your **conclusion**, <u>**before**</u> you start writing.

11. Brainstorm the **relevant points** and write these down in rough in the form of a spider diagram. Write these directly on your question paper. The examiner will review any rough notes made if you run out of time.

12. Prioritise the order in which the above points will be discussed. Write a number next to each point in the order that you intend to discuss them.

13. Introduce your answer – explain how you intend to answer the question, show that you have understood the question.

14. Discuss **more than one point** in depth, consider **more than one side** to an argument.

15. Keep **referring back** to the original question set <u>and</u> the business in the question **throughout** your answer.

16. Consider the possible **advantages** or **disadvantages** and / or the **implications / impact / effect** of any problems, issues or solutions being considered on the business – always referring to evidence presented in the question / data response material.

17. Always try to **conclude** each question – What do you consider to be the **most important, significant, relevant** point your have made and ***why*** is it for **this particular business?** *What* should be done in the <u>short term</u>? <u>long term</u>? *Why?* Consider the **objectives** of the business, the **resources** available <u>and</u> the **likelihood of success** (taking into account the strengths and weaknesses of the business, and opportunities and threats), as applicable.

18. Have <u>**CONFIDENCE in YOURSELF**</u> – you now have a great deal of knowledge. ***Use*** this knowledge well!